5ᵗʰ Edition

Instructor's Resource Manual for Corey, Corey, & Callanan's

Issues *and* Ethics
in the Helping Professions

Gerald Corey
California State University, Fullerton
Diplomate in Counseling Psychology,
American Board of Professional Psychology

Marianne Schneider Corey
Private Practice

Patrick Callanan
Private Practice

Mary Lou O'Phelan
Century College

BROOKS/COLE PUBLISHING COMPANY
I**T**P® An International Thomson Publishing Company

Pacific Grove • Albany • Belmont • Bonn • Boston • Cincinnati
Detroit • Johannesburg • London • Madrid • Melbourne • Mexico City
New York • Paris • Singapore • Tokyo • Toronto • Washington

For more information, contact:

BROOKS/COLE PUBLISHING COMPANY
511 Forest Lodge Road
Pacific Grove, CA 93950
USA

International Thomson Editores
Seneca 53
Col. Polanco
11560 México, D. F., México

International Thomson Publishing Europe
Berkshire House 168-173
High Holborn
London WC1V 7AA
England

International Thomson Publishing GmbH
Königswinterer Strasse 418
53227 Bonn
Germany

Thomas Nelson Australia
102 Dodds Street
South Melbourne, 3205
Victoria, Australia

International Thomson Publishing Asia
221 Henderson Road
#05-10 Henderson Building
Singapore 0315

Nelson Canada
1120 Birchmount Road
Scarborough, Ontario
Canada M1K 5G4

International Thomson Publishing Japan
2-2-1 Hirakawacho
Chiyoda-ku, Tokyo 102
Japan

Printed in the United States of America

5   4   3   2   1

ISBN 0-534-35053-4

TABLE OF CONTENTS

PREFACE

We appreciate you adopting *Issues and Ethics in the Helping Professions, Fifth Edition,* and we sincerely hope that you and your students will find it a useful tool for promoting reflection and discussion on a range of significant issues.

In this manual we begin by offering some perspectives on teaching courses dealing with ethical and professional issues. The discussion focuses on assisting students in developing an ethical sense, the role of modeling of attitudes and behaviors on the part of the faculty, ways of teaching ethical decision making, surveys on the practices of teaching graduate courses in ethics, and trends in the teaching of ethics.

A sample course outline then follows, with detailed writing assignments, schedule of topics and assignments for a semester course, and guidelines for students in getting the most from the course.

The next section consists of a study guide for *Issues and Ethics in the Helping Professions, Fifth Edition.* There are some key questions to guide students in their reading and reviewing of each chapter. You may want to use some of these questions as catalysts for class discussion, for take-home written assignments, for small-group interaction, or for test questions. The questions highlight the core ideas of each chapter and also ask for student reaction to some topics. These questions can be included as part of the course syllabus.

The following section includes chapter quizzes for all thirteen chapters. These can be used to test the student weekly or combined to meet your criteria for testing. These questions were written to test the student's knowledge of the facts and concepts included in each chapter. There are also case study questions to test the student's ability to apply the knowledge learned through their readings and experiential exercises done in the classroom.

The last section is a final examination, which consists of 150 objective test items based on *Issues and Ethics in the Helping Professions, Fifth Edition.* Let us know how the book works for you and your students. You can contact Jerry and Marianne Corey at P.O. Box 2038, Idyllwild, CA 92549 or by phone at (909) 659-4320 and Patrick Callanan at (714) 493-5064. You can also FAX the Corey's at (909) 659-6117. Their e-mail is cordileone@aol.com.

PERSPECTIVES ON THE TEACHING OF ETHICS

What follows is some material that we hope instructors will find useful in designing an ethics course and in developing a course outline. Some of the following material can be included in a course outline or in a handout that is given to students at the beginning of the course. We focus on the role of faculty modeling and also explore some of the goals of teaching ethics. Since there are different approaches to presenting an ethics course, we summarize some perspectives on the teaching of ethics, and highlight some trends in the field.

The Formation of an Ethical Sense

For students, developing an ethical sense includes committing themselves to their education, being an active learner, learning from role models such as their professors, and getting involved in related course work. From our perspective the cultivation of an ethical sense begins with students' commitment to their education in the helping professions. The way they approach their education has a bearing on the way they will approach their professional career. If they are committed to their studies on both an intellectual and emotional level, they will probably bring this enthusiasm and dedication to their professional practice. Of course, there are those students who are committed to manipulating the system so that they can merely get by with minimal effort. Some take the shortest route to earning a degree and getting a license, and once they attain these goals, they stop learning. We are convinced that these people are limited in their capacity to help others.

In addition to being active learners, it is essential, we think, that students be aware of their motivations for choosing the helping professions as a career. The motivations for being a helper are related to the development of an ethical sense. Although many personal needs can be met through helping others, it is crucial that these needs not be met at the expense of the client. Those who make a lifetime commitment to helping others have a responsibility to be clear about what they are getting from their work and how their personal characteristics play a vital role in their ability to make appropriate ethical decisions.

1

Note: The bibliographic references indicated in the sections below can be found in the References on pages 6–7.

Role of Faculty Modeling in Teaching Students Ethics

We contend that the faculty of any program in the helping professions plays a major role in modeling an ethical sense. The ways in which the faculty members teach their courses and relate to and supervise students have a significant impact. For example, supervisors may model confidentiality—or the lack of it—by how they talk about their own clients. As Kitchener (1984) has pointed out, one way of teaching students what it means to be an ethical professional is by being truthful, honest, and direct with them. The faculty members must be open to honest self-exploration of the ethical issues they face if they hope to have an impact on their students' ability to think from an ethical perspective. Kitchener (1986) puts this matter well:

> By modeling, through discussions, and by valuing ethical behavior, counselor educators can encourage young professionals to develop a sense of responsibility to act in an ethically responsible manner. Also, they can help them learn to tolerate the ambiguity involved in ethical decision making. First, however, counselor educators must learn to tolerate ambiguity themselves [1986, p. 310].

We agree with the contention of Engels, Wilborn, and Schneider (1990) concerning the importance of professors and supervisors taking the risks involved in good learning and good counseling practice. They see it as imperative that faculty members engage in ongoing self-examination regarding personal and professional values, ethics, competence, and dedication. They emphasize that the best route to teaching these characteristics is by their modeling. Our students are likely to be more influenced by what we are actually doing than by what we say others should be doing.

According to Tabachnick, Keith-Spiegel, and Pope (1991), there has been a lack of comprehensive and systematic data concerning the beliefs and behaviors of psychologists who function as educators. Their study was based on the assumption that there is a need to research which aspects of teaching are viewed as presenting ethical dilemmas for psychologists, how often those dilemmas occur, and how psychologists respond to the ethical issues they face as educators. Survey data were collected from psychologists who worked in higher education. They were asked the degree to which they engaged in 63 behaviors and the degree to which they considered each of these to be ethical. Of these 63 behaviors, 6 were very difficult for

2

participants to evaluate on the basis of ethics, and 10 were exceptionally controversial. Based on the outcomes of their survey, Tabachnick et al. concluded that psychologists who serve as educators could benefit by a process of ethical self-examination and accountability. They encouraged psychologists to model through their teaching the self-reflection on ethical issues that they expect of their students. The authors stated, "A crucial aspect of the maturation and moral development of any profession is the collective openness and dedication of its membership to study and critically examine itself" (p. 515). They suggest that it is time for psychologists to bring the strategies and rigorous discipline of psychology to their own behavior and beliefs as teachers.

Ways of Teaching Ethical Decision Making

Kitchener (1986) has suggested that ethics training should create sensitivity to the ethical issues in the profession and to the implications of professional actions; should improve the ability to reason about ethical issues; should instill the determination to act in ethical ways; and should teach tolerance of ambiguity in ethical decision making as opposed to rigid indoctrination of "right" and "wrong."

We endorse the practice of teaching students the process of making ethical decisions from the very beginning of their training program. The teaching of ethics can be conceptualized as progressing from a focus on theoretical issues to a stress on practical issues. When students are introduced to ethics education, it is likely that the emphasis will be on teaching general principles of ethical reasoning. Specific application can involve creating situations in the classroom in which students are challenged to apply ethical principles to specific cases.

Our Approach to the Teaching of Ethics

Two of us (Patrick Callanan and Gerald Corey) regularly co-teach an ethics course for undergraduate students in the Human Services Department at California State University, Fullerton. Rather than rely on lecture methods, we do our best to involve our students in identifying and examining the basic ethical principles involved in a variety of ethical dilemmas. Toward the goal of increasing student involvement, we do a good deal of role playing and dramatizing vignettes. Frequently, we assume the role of devil's advocate and challenge students to come up with reasons for whatever position they might assume. We ask our students to bring their concerns about the issues in the assigned readings. As much as possible, we attempt

3

to facilitate interaction and discussion within the classroom. Our hope is that students will develop an appreciation for the value of thinking through ethical dilemmas by examining their own motivations and values. We ask students to be alert to the subtle ways that they might be ethically insensitive at times. We consistently encourage them to focus on their own motivations and behavior, rather than developing a judgmental stance by critiquing the ethics of others. Although many of our students do not have much practical experience in the field, we typically bring in practical examples and dilemmas that we expect they may eventually encounter. Through feedback from our students, we typically find case vignettes to be an effective way of developing decision-making attitudes and skills.

Teaching at the Graduate Level

Graduate courses in ethics at both the beginning and the end of the program are an ideal way to provide students with opportunities to grapple with ethical principles and apply them to practice. What are some practices in the teaching of ethics? A national survey of 289 master's programs in psychology assessed the type of ethics training that was available (Handelsman, 1986a). The results of this survey indicated that 87% of these programs had some format for teaching ethics; 29% had a formal and separate course in ethics; 47% taught ethics as a part of a formal course; and 11% dealt with ethical issues in informal ways through discussion during practicum and internship supervision sessions. Although 98.5% of the respondents believed that ethics could be taught adequately at the master's level, only 57% of them would recommend a formal course devoted entirely to ethics. Handelsman concluded that ethical thinking should be regarded as a skill, which can and ought to be taught in formal courses. Engels, Wilborn, and Schneider (1990) believe that ethics education is best taught in an ongoing way and that ethics can be infused in every aspect of the program. They favor including a didactic course in ethics and professional issues as a means of pulling together threads from many diverse aspects of training and for presenting aggregate information in a systematic and formal way.

Lipsitz (1985) reports that the literature reveals a sevenfold increase in the availability of training experiences over the last 30 years. It appears that both formal and integrated ethics training are well respected by students who have been exposed to them. Ninety-two percent of the participants in the Lipsitz study were exposed to some systematic attempt to incorporate the topic of professional ethics into their curriculum. Of this group, 51% had a formal course in ethics, and 41% received ethics training that was integrated throughout their program.

Handelsman (1986b) presents a persuasive case for reconceptualizing ethics education. Contending that there are problems with ethics training by "osmosis," he maintains that ethical thinking is a skill that must be developed through formal courses devoted primarily to ethics. For him, relying exclusively on informal methods alone, such as teaching ethics in the context of supervision, is a dangerous practice.

As Welfel and Lipsitz (1984) point out, however, more research is needed to determine the impact of formal course work in ethics. These authors contend that the literature only very weakly supports the interpretation that ethics courses have a positive impact on students. There is no study dealing with the influence of ethics training on actual behavior with clients. There are also no data to determine whether ethics is better taught in a separate course or integrated into existing courses in the curriculum. Welfel and Lipsitz raise the question of whether knowing ethical codes and learning a way of thinking and dealing with ethical dilemmas will actually be translated into actual practice. They acknowledge that progress has been made over the last 30 years in ethics education, but they ask if this increased attention to ethics training says much about the quality of this training. They assert that ethics courses are likely to fall short of their ultimate goals despite the best intentions of those who teach them.

Trends in the Teaching of Ethics

The process of learning to become an ethical practitioner begins with counselor-education programs, which normally include seminars in ethical principles and practices. Students should, as a beginning, thoroughly familiarize themselves with established ethical standards. They need to be sensitive to any ethical problems that arise in their practicum experiences and then discuss the problems in a seminar session or consult their supervisor. Part of a counselor's training is developing a sense of sound judgment, and dealing with basic ethical issues can assist in that development. Fortunately, there is a clear trend toward introducing counselors-in-training to the kinds of ethical and legal issues that they are likely to encounter. In reviewing the state of ethical training for counseling psychology doctoral students, Wilson and Ranft (1993) concluded that ethics training in graduate psychology programs has blossomed in the last decade. The results of their survey indicated that 94% of counseling psychology programs require training in ethics. Students in these programs feel prepared for both ethical and legal issues that are likely to arise in their professional roles. They claim that they feel more prepared in the decision-making process than in factual information of ethics.

The increased interest given to ethics education is related to an increase in malpractice litigation. The greater consciousness in the human-services professions about ethical and legal responsibilities parallels a concurrent rise in public consciousness about legal rights. There is a great deal of professional concern over identifying appropriate actions in the face of conflicting ethical, legal, and professional demands (Haas, Malouf, & Mayerson, 1986).

Most of the attention has been given to violations of confidentiality and to sexual intimacies with clients. Other types of unethical behaviors have been documented, however, such as misrepresentation of skills, problems in the methods of collecting fees, improper use of assessment techniques, faulty diagnosis, treatment error, failure to respect client integrity, inappropriate public statements, violation of civil rights, assault and battery, and unethical research practices (Lipsitz, 1985; Pope, 1986).

A trend that we would like to see in the teaching of ethics is for educators to demonstrate a willingness to engage in open discussion with their students about their own ethical beliefs. We would also hope that educators would realize the value of teaching ethical behavior through the process of modeling ethical practices by the way they relate to students in their classes.

It is our view that formal course work in ethics, both in separate courses and through an integrated approach with the rest of the curriculum, will significantly help students benefit from supervised fieldwork. The course work can alert students to ethical, legal, and professional issues that they might not have looked for, and they will be able to bring to their fieldwork questions about the ethical dimensions of their practice.

References

Engels, D., Wilborn, B. L., & Schneider, L. J. (1990). Ethics curricula for counselor preparation programs. In B. Herlihy, & L. B. Golden (Eds.), *AACD ethical standards casebook* (4th ed.) (pp. 111–126). Alexandria, VA: American Association for Counseling and Development.

Haas, L. J., Malouf, J. L., & Mayerson, N. H. (1986). Ethical dilemmas in psychological practice: Results of a national survey. *Professional Psychology: Research and Practice, 17*(4), 316–321.

Handelsman, M. M. (1986a). Ethics training at the master's level: A national survey. *Professional Psychology: Research and Practice,* 17(1), 24–26.

Handelsman, M. M. (1986b). Problems with ethics training by "osmosis." *Professional Psychology: Research and Practice,* 17(4), 371–372.

Kitchener, K.S. (1984). Intuition, critical evaluation and ethical principles: The foundation for ethical decisions in counseling psychology. *The Counseling Psychologist,* 12(3), 43–55.

Kitchener, K.S. (1986). Teaching applied ethics in counselor education: An integration of psychological processes and philosophical analysis. *Journal of Counseling and Development,* 64(5), 306–310.

Lipsitz, N. E. (1985). *The relationship between ethics training and ethical discrimination ability.* Paper presented at the annual meeting of the American Psychological Association, Los Angeles.

Pope, K. S. (1986). New trends in malpractice cases and changes in APA's liability insurance. *Independent Practitioner,* 6(4), 23–26.

Tabachnick, B. G., Keith-Spiegel, P., & Pope, K. S. (1991). Ethics of teaching: Beliefs and behaviors of psychologists as educators. *American Psychologist,* 46(5), 506–515.

Weifel, E. R., & Lipsitz, N. E. (1984). The ethical behavior of professional psychologists: A critical analysis of the research. *The Counseling Psychologist,* 12(3), 31–42.

Wilson, L. S., & Ranft, V. A. (1993). The state of ethical training for counseling psychology doctoral students. *The Counseling Psychologist,* 21(3), 445–456.

COURSE OUTLINE FOR ETHICAL AND PROFESSIONAL ISSUES

HUMAN SERVICES 400

ETHICAL AND PROFESSIONAL ISSUES IN HUMAN SERVICES

Dr. Jerry Corey, Professor of Human Services and Counseling

Tuesday and Thursday: 11:30 to 12:45

Office Hours: Tuesdays 2:15 to 3:00 and Wednesdays 10:00 to 11:45; by prior appointment; and open office hour on Thursdays 1:00 to 2:00. Other times by prior appointment. Human Services Office phone is 773-3926. Home phone: (909) 659-4320.

Required Textbooks for Huser 400:

- Corey, G., Corey, M., and Callanan, P. (1998). *Issues and Ethics in the Helping Professions (5th ed.)*. Pacific Grove, CA: Brooks/Cole.
- Herlihy, B., & Corey, G. (1996). *ACA Ethical Standards Casebook*. ACA Publication.
- Herlihy, B., & Corey, G. (1997). *Bondary Issues in Counseling: Multiple Roles and Responsibilities*.

Recommended:

- *Hatherleigh Guide to Ethics in Therapy*. (1997). Hatherleigh Publishing Company.
- Selected Journal Articles (Distributed in class)

Course Description: Prerequisites: Huser 380 and 396; and Philosophy 310 *or* consent of instructor. A survey of the ethical, legal, and professional issues facing the human services worker. Designed to teach a process of ethical decision making and to increase awareness of the complexities in practice.

9

Objectives of the Course: Main goal of the course is to stimulate you to think about major issues related to sound and professional practice in human services and to challenge you to formulate a position on issues. You are expected to become familiar with the ethical codes of the counseling profession and to develop an increased ability to apply these ethical principles to a variety of specific problem situations that will be discussed in class.

Schedule: HUMAN SERVICES 400

WEEKS TOPICS FOR DISCUSSION AND ASSIGNED READINGS

Week 1
:   **Introduction to Professional Ethics**
    Chapter 1: Self-Inventory (Discuss in class)
    Video: ACA's Tele-Conference on Ethics in Counseling

Week 2
:   **Counselor and Person and as Professional**
    Analysis and Discussion of Ethical Codes (Appendix)
    Review all the Codes in Appendix (ACA Ethical Standards)
    Complete Chapter 2: **The Counselor as a Person and as a Professional**

Week 3
:   Chapter 3: **Values and the Helping Relationship**
    Dr. Thomas Parham Workshop at CSUF
    Workshop on Multicultural Perspectives

Week 4
:   Chapter 4: **Client Rights and Counselor Responsibilities**
    Legal Issues and Malpractice Concerns
    ACA Casebook (Read selected essays on above topics)
    ACA Video (Part on Informed Consent and Confidentiality)

Week 5
:   Chapter 5: **Confidentiality: Ethical and Legal Issues**
    ACA Casebook (Read selected essays on above topics)
    Duty to Warn/Protect & Court Cases

Week 6
:   Chapter 6: **Theory, Practice, and Research**
    ACA Casebook (Read selected essays on above topics)

    - **Paper #1 due**

Week 7	Chapter 7: **Managing Boundaries and Multiple Relationships** **ACA Video** (Part on Dual Relationships)
Week 8	**Boundary Issues in Counseling: Multiple Roles and Relationships** Reading due: Herlihy & Corey: *Boundary Issues in Counseling* Chapter 7: (*Issues and Ethics* text — Continued)
Week 9	**Boundary Issues** (continued) Focus on Herlihy & Corey book, *Boundary Issues in Counseling*
Week 10	Chapter 8: **Professional Competence and Training Video:** Art of Integrated Psychotherapy (Part I)
Week 11	Chapter 9: **Issues in Supervision and Consultation** **ACA Casebook** (Read selected essays on above topics)
Week 12	Chapter 10: **Multicultural Perspectives and Diversity Issues** and **ACA Casebook** **ACA Video** (Part on Ethics in Multicultural Counseling)
Week 13	Chapter 11: **The Counselor in the Community** [Read *Boundary Issues* book on Community]
Week 14	Chapter 12: **Ethics in Marriage and Family Therapy** • **Paper #2 due** • Focus discussion on **AAMFT Ethical Standards** **ACA Casebook**
Week 15	Chapter 13: **Ethics in Group Counseling and Review of Issues and Evaluation** Retake the Self-Inventory in Chapter 1 and discuss in class. Discuss impact of course and key issues.

11

Focus of the Ethics Course

The class will *not* be a lecture class, rather it will be conducted more along the lines of a *seminar*. While some brief lectures will be given, the focus is upon discussion, interaction, role-playing, exploration of issues, and carrying out in class (and small groups) the *activities and exercises* at the end of each chapter. On Tuesdays, this class will be co-taught by Patrick Callanan and Jerry Corey. For diversity, there will be a few guest speakers. Come to class prepared! Read, think, be willing to state your views, exchange ideas!

We hope you'll use any fieldwork experience as a basis for identifying ethical and professional issues that you want to discuss in class. The readings and discussions will "come alive" for you if you can relate these topics to issues you have experienced and struggled with in a practicum or fieldwork placement. Above all, relax and enjoy the challenge of this course! We most hope that you will become intellectually and emotionally engaged and give the course your best effort. Please arrange time to see either of the instructors out of class if you want to talk about anything that results from your being enrolled in the course.

Grading Practices and Policy

Your grade for this course will be determined by evidence of the quality of your learning as demonstrated by your performance on the following areas:

(1) *Paper #1* will count as one-third of your course grade.
(2) *Paper #2* will count as one-third of your course grade.
(3) *FINAL EXAMINATION* (which is a comprehensive sample of major issues in the entire course), will count as one-third of your grade. The final consists of 200 objective-type questions from two texts, *Issues and Ethics in the Helping Professions* and *ACA Ethics Casebook*.

Note: Be sure to bring TEXTBOOK, Readings, and this COURSE OUTLINE to each of the classes.

Class Participation: This course is organized in a seminar format and you are expected to participate in the class activities and discussions. Your final course grade may be affected by both the quality and quantity of your in-

12

class participation and attendance. If you are not willing to become an active participant, do not enroll in the course.

ATTENDANCE is expected at each class meeting, unless you have an emergency situation or are really ill. For me to credit you with an EXCUSED ABSENCE, you need to know that it is YOUR RESPONSIBILITY to inform me of such cases immediately upon returning to class. Absences will be a factor in determining your participation/attendance grade; excessive absences might result in getting a full grade deducted (or in some cases even failing the course). While I do not mean to be petty about this issue, I do expect you to function as a professional in any agency, which means showing up and participating!

Grading Scale (percentage) is as follows:

100–98 = A+
97–94 = A
93–91 = A-
90–88 = B+
87–84 = B
83–81 = B-
80–78 = C+
77–74 = C
73–71 = C-
70–68 = D+
67–64 = D
63–61 = D-
Below 60 = F

A curve is not used for grading in this course. Students who choose to remain in this course until the end tend to do well. The grade of "A" is reserved for exception performance in all of the areas of the course.

Guidelines for Paper #1 and Paper #2 for Huser 400

PAPERS #1 AND #2 make up **two-thirds** of your course grade. *LATE PAPERS* generally have a **penalty of at least** -10% to -15% deduction (if only a few days late) from the total. They should be TYPED and double-spaced, CAREFULLY PROOFREAD, and should give evidence of considerable thought/outside reading, and must show a development of your positions in a coherent, logical, and organized way.

FOR PAPER #1 select **five questions** (from the topics explored up to the date this paper is due). For the first paper, write a two-page essay on each of the following topics:

(1) Take an ethical dilemma and show how you would resolve this dilemma by using one of the ethical decision-making models.
(2) A Value Issue: How Your Values May Affect Your Counseling
(3) A Client Rights Issues
(4) Some Dimension of Confidentiality
(5) Some topic from Chapters 1 to 5 (Other than any of the topics specified above)

For PAPER #2 select **four** other questions (from the topics from the latter portion of the course: Chapters 6 through 13). Select questions that are challenging to you and ones that will help you think through your position. Question #5 is a self-evaluation paper.

We hope that your papers will be done in personal style and will reflect the end result of your study/research review/thought on given ethical and professional issues. *Each essay is to be about 2 pages in length (double-spaced).* (Each paper is 10 pages in length). Each week you should keep up to date in writing the rough drafts for your position papers. Select a topic weekly and make an outline and rough draft while your thoughts are fresh. Do the critiques of the chapters on a weekly basis. Writing a rough draft as you go along will insure greater clarity. In the long run, it will save time and much frustration on your part. You should know that you are not graded on your viewpoints and thoughts as such. Instead, your grade is a function of your ability to clearly and fully express your ideas. We are looking for depth of thinking, originality, critical evaluation, the ability to apply theories to practical situations, independent judgment, organization, and insights into issues. Let your papers demonstrate that you are doing the reading and reflecting necessary to produce a quality paper.

Question #5: Self-Evaluation Paper

1. What do you consider to be the *most significant learnings* for you that grew out of this course? List them in order. Then, select a few of them and discuss *how* those learnings were of significance and why.

2. What questions have you raised this semester? What questions have particularly stood out for you with the readings, the speakers, the class discussions, and the lectures?

3. How would you *evaluate yourself* as a learner in this course? Specifically, assess yourself on all dimensions: What was the quality of your papers? How much of yourself did you invest in this course? How would you assess your class participation? How involved were you? How much did you risk? What did you contribute to the class? How critically and thoughtfully did you do the assigned readings? Did you do any outside reading? If so, what?

Questions for Papers #1 and #2

Your task is to *narrow down* a question so that you have a clear focus, to take a definite position and develop it fully and cogently, and to give logical reasons for your perspectives. To write outstanding papers, it will help to show evidence that you have read the relevant material in the textbook, *and* that you have done *some supplementary reading* on each issue in question (specific journal articles, or chapters and readings from the *ACA Ethical Standards Casebook),* and from the *Boundary Issues* book, *and* that you have drawn upon any experiences that you have encountered in your *practicum or fieldwork* placements. We suggest that you select topics that you are struggling with or have experienced in your field placements. To give your discussion some added force, it is recommended that you integrate some ideas taken from selected readings in the textbooks.

We are interested in challenging you to develop your own positions and the ability to back up these views with supporting evidence (either through your observations and experiences, or through a survey of views from other writers). These are to be THOUGHT PAPERS, not merely summary of information papers! Take a SPECIFIC position, show *why* you take such a position, and then develop your viewpoints by giving *reasons* for the statements you make.

Suggestions for Writing and Criteria for Grading

1. *Quality writing skills.* Write directly and informally, yet write in standard English. I encourage you to use personal examples and to support your points with these examples when appropriate. Make sure your essays reflect university-level writing skills. Use complete sentences, develop your

paragraphs, check your spelling, and put together a paper that reflects quality. You might ask someone to proofread your paper.

- It is essential that you keep strictly within the established page limitations.

2. **Development of a theme.** Look for a central theme or central message in each essay. Make an outline, and check to see that each point in your outline pertains to your central message.

- Create a short title for each essay that conveys your basic idea.
- State your message concisely in your opening paragraph.
- Have a solid and impactful concluding paragraph.
- The theme should be clear, concise, and specific—rather than global and generalized. Do not write in a general and abstract manner, or else your essays will lose a clear focus.
- Develop your thoughts fully, concretely, and logically—rather than rambling or being vague and wordy.
- In terms of form and organization, your paper should flow well, and your points should relate to one another. The reader should not have to struggle to discover your intended meaning.
- Give reasons for your views—rather than making unsupported statements. In taking a position, provide reasons for your position.
- Cover a few issues or ideas well and in depth, rather than spreading yourself too thin. For each essay, narrow down your question or topic so that you can manage to develop central paragraphs that expand on your theme.

3. **Use of examples.** In developing your ideas, use clear examples to illustrate your point. Draw upon personal examples, use cases, and apply theoretical concepts to practical settings. Tie your examples into the point you are making—but avoid giving too many details or getting lost in the personal example.

4. **Creativity and depth of thinking.** Write a paper that reflects your own uniqueness and ideas—rather than merely giving a summary of the material in the book.

- Approach the material in an original way.

- Focus on a particular issue or topic that you find personally significant. Since you have a choice in what aspect to focus on, select an aspect of a problem that will allow you to express your beliefs.
- Show depth in expanding on your thoughts.

5. *Integration and application.* Your papers should emphasize an integration of perspectives and application of theory/principles to practice.

- Demonstrate that you know the material or the issues involved through an integration and synthesis of theories, accurate understanding of theoretical concepts, critical evaluation of theories, and ability to apply ideas to practical situations.

- If you are writing a theory essay, focus on those specific aspects of the theory that you'd most like to incorporate into your own style of counseling. Stress the implications for counseling practice. Rather than writing merely about a theoretical issue, show how this issue has meaning in a counseling situation.

- Apply your ideas to specific populations that you expect to work with— both in counseling and non-counseling situations. You may want to apply your essays to teaching, working with the elderly, working in corrections, working with adolescents, etc. Make these a personal and meaningful experience.

- In writing about ethical issues, be sure to zero in on a specific message. What do you most want to convey?

- In writing about a case, be sure to show that you can apply several approaches or perspectives to this case. Work with the case by attempting to combine a number of perspectives.

Review of Course: Perspectives on Ethical and Professional Issues

1. Retake and review the *self-inventory* in *Chapter 1.* Circle those items that you've noticed any changes in your way of thinking. Bring in a few items you'd most like to talk about in small groups.

2. Retake and review the *self-inventories* at the beginning of *each* of the chapters. Notice any changes in your perspectives?

3. If you were to apply for a job as a mental health worker, or to a graduate school, and the interviewer stated the following, how would you respond?

"I notice you had a course in ethical and professional issues. Tell me how that course has prepared you to more effectively meet the challenges you might face on this job (or in this graduate program)."

4.   You've worked with the textbook, *Issues and Ethics in the Helping Professions* all semester. Give a specific assessment of how the book fit for this course. What has been the overall impact of the supplementary readings on you? What topics and issues had the *most* impact on you and *why?*

5.   If you were asked to select the ONE most significant question, and then to *discuss your own question,* what would be your question? And, answer the question, or at least discuss the issue.

6.   Discuss the ways that the entire course, and all aspects of it, have influenced you both *as a person* and *as a future professional.*

7.   Review your *self-evaluation paper.* What are some of the most significant learnings for you this semester? How would you evaluate yourself as a learner in this course?

Final Essay Examination for Huser 400
5 questions—each worth 10 points

1.   Assume that you have just graduated with a BS in Human Services and you secure a position as a mental health worker in a community agency. During your first week at this agency, your supervisor asks you to work with a family who is having a great deal of difficulty with two of their five children. You have had no training and no course work in family therapy, so being ethical, you tell your supervisor that you cannot ethically work with this family at this time.
  Your supervisor argues that you are lacking in confidence, yet you feel strongly that if you accept the assignment that it would be unethical. Briefly describe the specific steps that you would take in dealing with this ETHICAL conflict between you and your supervisor.

2.   Assume that you are working in a community agency with client populations with diverse ethnic and cultural backgrounds from yourself. You are hired to provide individual, group, marital, and family counseling to a wide range of clients. From an ETHICAL perspective, what would you

need to do to increase your chances of providing effective counseling services to your culturally different clients?

3.   The issue of HIV/AIDS will continue to present a number of challenges to mental-health professionals. Identify and discuss what you consider to be some of the most pressing ETHICAL concerns that you may struggle with as a practitioner in dealing with this issue.

4.   The role of your values as a counselor will be particularly crucial if you provide either *family therapy* or do *group counseling.* Select ONE value that you are committed to that is likely to influence the way you work with a family (or the way you facilitate a group). Apply this value to either a group *or* to a family situation, identifying what you consider to be the ETHICAL dimensions of working with your values in this specific situation. How will your values influence the direction you take with a family or with a group?

5.   The chances are great that you will work in a community agency. Identify what you consider to be a few of the major challenges that you expect to face as a counselor in working in the community. How would you reach those who most need your professional assistance? What are the ETHICAL implications of dealing with the challenges that you have identified?

STUDENT EVALUATION OF THE COURSE AND THE INSTRUCTOR

Student Evaluation of the Instructor

Read each statement below that describes some facet of the instructor. Decide the degree to which you agree or disagree with each of the following statements about the instructor of this course. Use the following code:

     5 = I *strongly agree* with this statement.
     4 = I *agree,* in most respects, with this statement.
     3 = I am *undecided* in my opinion about this statement.
     2 = I *disagree,* in most respects, with this statement.
     1 = I *strongly disagree* with this statement.

THE INSTRUCTOR OF THIS COURSE:

_____ 1. demonstrates a broad and accurate knowledge of most of the subjects in this course.
_____ 2. clearly presents the subject matter.
_____ 3. effectively adjusts to my level of comprehension.
_____ 4. enjoys teaching and has a high degree of enthusiasm.
_____ 5. welcomes differences of opinions.
_____ 6. demonstrates a respectful attitude toward students.
_____ 7. stimulates the intellectual curiosity of the students.
_____ 8. uses appropriate and useful teaching methods.
_____ 9. demonstrates an understanding and accepting attitude toward students.
_____ 10. provides an encouraging and supportive climate in the classroom.
_____ 11. invites students to seek personal help as a way of getting the most from the course.
_____ 12. clearly presents the objectives of the course.
_____ 13. is well-organized and utilizes class time effectively.
_____ 14. gives relevant and helpful out-of-class assignments.
_____ 15. is clear about the criteria for grading.
_____ 16. demonstrates fairness in determining grades.

_____ 17. creates a classroom atmosphere that is extremely helpful to learning.
_____ 18. addresses students' concerns and seems genuinely interested in students' progress in this course.
_____ 19. is friendly both in and out of class.
_____ 20. consistently abides by the policies and procedures as described in the course outline.

Evaluation of Course and Instructor

Please put in the blank the letter of the statement which you believe to be most true of this course or this instructor for each topic.

_____ 1. To what degree do you feel the objectives of this course were met?
a. All of the important goals were met.
b. Many of the goals were attained.
c. Some of the goals were attained.
d. Many of the goals were not attained.
e. The important goals were not attained.

_____ 2. How much actual work and study outside of class did you do for this course?
a. Much more than for most of my courses.
b. More than for my other courses.
c. About the same as for my other courses.
d. Less than for most of my courses.

_____ 3. How valuable was the textbook to you?
a. Outstanding in value.
b. Almost all part were valuable.
c. Generally valuable.
d. Some parts worth reading.
e. A waste of time.

_____ 4. How does the instructor of this course compare with instructors in other college courses you have taken?
   a. One of the best.
   b. Better than most.
   c. About the same as most.
   d. Worse than most.
   e. One of the worst.

_____ 5. This course has been:
   a. extremely challenging.
   b. very challenging.
   c. somewhat challenging.
   d. not too challenging.
   e. extremely unchallenging.

_____ 6. Compared with other classes, this class has been:
   a. much more interesting.
   b. more interesting.
   c. about as interesting.
   d. less interesting.
   e. much less interesting.

_____ 7. As far as learning material that will be of practical use in my college career and my life, this course has been:
   a. very helpful
   b. somewhat helpful.
   c. not too helpful.

_____ 8. Would you recommend this course, in terms of its content, to a good friend whose interests are like yours?
   a. Yes, recommend it highly.
   b. Yes, it is better than most courses.
   c. Undecided.
   d. No, it is not as good as most courses.

_____ 9. Would you recommend this instructor to a good friend?
   a. Yes, recommend the instructor highly.
   b. Yes, the instructor is better than most.
   c. Undecided.
   d. No, the instructor is not as good as most.

23

_____ 10. What overall rating would you give to this instructor?
   a. Superior.
   b. Very good.
   c. Good.
   d. Fair
   e. Poor.

_____ 11. What overall rating would you give to this course?
   a. Superior.
   b. Very good.
   c. Good.
   d. Fair
   e. Poor.

_____ 12. How would you assess the value of what you have learned from this course?
   a. Learned or gained a great deal from this class.
   b. Learned or gained enough from this class to make it worth the time.
   c. Learned or gained little from this class.
   d. Learned or gained almost nothing from this class.

   For the following questions, please write a brief statement that reflects your honest view.

13. What topics in this course did you find most meaningful and of most value to you personally?

14. What topics in this course did you find least meaningful?

15. What other topic(s) would you like to see included in this course?

16. Which of your personal or academic concerns were not adequately addressed in this course?

17. Which assignments stand out as being most valuable to you?

18. To what degree has this course been useful in giving you ideas and tools that you can apply to all of your other courses?

19. To what degree did you read, study, and reflect on the material in the textbook?

20. Please make any other comments you wish or list any other suggestions for improving the course. And thank you for taking the time to complete this evaluation in an honest manner.

STUDY GUIDE for
Issues and Ethics in the Helping Professions, Fifth Edition

CHAPTER 1—Introduction to Professional Ethics

Ethical Decision Making

1. Be familiar with the meaning of the following terms and the differences among these terms: ethics, values, morality, community standards, laws, and professionalism.

2. What is the relationship between law and ethics? What might you do if you were faced with a conflict between a legal standard and an ethical principle?

3. Differentiate between mandatory ethics and aspirational ethics.

4. What is the role of professional codes? How do codes of ethics help counselors? What are the limitations of these codes?

5. What are some problems with the enforcement of ethical codes?

6. What are the differences between principle ethics and virtue ethics?

7. One model of ethical decision making is based on these six basic moral principles: autonomy, nonmaleficence, beneficence, justice, fidelity, and veracity. Be able to define each concept and provide an example for each principle.

8. Select an ethical dilemma and apply systematic steps to the resolution of the dilemma. Show the steps you might use in making an ethical decision. How might you include a client in making such a decision?

9. What are some of the advantages of including the client in the process of working through ethical decisions? Discuss the feminist model of ethical

decision making, showing how some of the ideas of this model can lead to client empowerment.

10. If a professional disagrees with a particular ethical standard, and decides to practice in a way that is not sanctioned by an association, what are the consequences for that practitioner?

11. The text states that you need to develop an ethical sense that will enable you to better serve the welfare of your clients. What are some ways that you can think of to best develop this ethical sense?

CHAPTER 2—The Counselor as a Person and as a Professional

Self-Awareness and Influence of Therapist's Personality and Needs

1. How do unresolved personal conflicts affect the counselor's ability to work with clients?

2. What are some of your major needs that you see as influencing you in becoming a counselor? How might your needs be met through your work?

3. If you were asked the question "What do you personally get from doing counseling?", how would you answer this in a job interview?

Issues of Personal Therapy for Counselors

1. What is the rationale for the premise that therapy is essential for therapists and for trainees?

2. Do you think that personal therapy should be required of all trainees in a counseling program? If so, why? And what form of therapy do you think should be required?

3. To what extent do therapists make use of therapy for themselves? For those practitioners who are reluctant to seek professional assistance for themselves when they are highly stressed, what do you think might account for this reluctance?

4. Do you think that therapy should be *required* for an impaired therapist?

Dealing with Transference and Countertransference

1. How can transference and countertransference be ethical issues?

2. In what way is transference an "unreal" relationship in therapy?

3. When is countertransference a problem? If you were to become aware of countertransference reactions toward a particular client, what course of action would you likely follow?

4. Identify some of the major ways that countertransference is likely to be manifested. What are some of the signs that a therapist is experiencing countertransference?

Client Dependence and Manipulation

1. In what sense is promoting client dependence an ethical issue? What are some examples of fostering client dependence?

2. How can delaying termination of therapy be a form of client dependency?

3. How is manipulation an ethical issue? Could it be said that manipulation is really a part of every therapy approach?

4. What are some ways that you can develop collaborative relationships with your clients?

Stress in the Counseling Profession

1. What are the major sources of stress for therapists?

2. How does the stress of professional practice impact the counselor's personal life? What are the ethical issues here?

3. What are some of your concerns about your ability to cope with the stresses associated with being a professional?

4. What is your concept of the impaired therapist? What suggestions would you have if an impaired colleague sought you out for help?

5. What is your personal strategy for keeping yourself alive as a person and as a professional?

CHAPTER 3—Values and the Helping Relationship

Clarifying Your Values and Value Conflicts with Clients

1. Is it possible for counselors to keep their values out of their counseling sessions? What are the various views on this issue?

2. What are the ethics of imposing counselor values on clients?

3. Do you think that there are times or circumstances where it is ethical for you to direct clients in a particular direction? What about instilling in clients certain basic values such as responsibility, avoiding harm to others, being honest with others, self-determination, developing the ability to give and receive affection, finding a sense of purpose, and living authentically?

4. You will inevitably incorporate certain value orientations into your therapeutic practice. What is the ethical obligation you have in informing clients about your value orientation? How might you do this in your practice?

5. Is it possible for you, as a therapist, to interact honestly with your clients without making value judgments? Do you see it as desirable to avoid making judgments in all circumstances?

6. Can you remain true to yourself and at the same time allow your clients the freedom to select their own values, even if they differ sharply from yours?

7. At what point are counselors ethically obligated to refer a client because of a conflict of values? When would you feel it necessary to refer?

8. Do counselors need to share the same life experiences and world views of their clients to effectively work with them? If you have a background that is quite different from your client, how will you be able to make a connection with him or her?

Role of Spiritual and Religious Values In Counseling

1.   Discuss the trend in the counseling profession that seems to be taking a stronger stand on incorporating spirituality and religion as a factor in assessment and treatment.

2.   The premise of the authors is that spiritual and religious values have a major part to play in human life, which means that exploring these values has a great deal to do with providing solutions to the client's struggles. What is your reaction to this premise?

3.   How would you expect your spiritual and religious values to affect the manner in which you counsel? Would you be inclined to introduce the topic of spirituality or religion if your client did not make specific mention of such factors, if you believed that doing so would be helpful?

4.   What are some ways that religion and spirituality in counseling might conflict? In what ways can the two work in concert? What is the interface between the values espoused by religion and spirituality within the framework of counseling practice?

5.   What are some reasons to include spiritual and religious values in counseling? What potential problems can you see with doing so?

6.   What is the responsibility of training programs in preparing future counselors to deal with the religious and spiritual concerns of their clients?

7.   What kind of competencies in spirituality do you think counselors should have by the end of their training?

End-of-Life Decisions

1.   What are the ethical considerations in the right to die and in suicide?

2.   If a person is able to make a free and rational choice about ending his or her life, do you think that the state should interfere in this choice?

3.   What are some of the arguments for and against physician-assisted suicide? What is the possible role that a counselor might assume in such cases?

31

4. What is the essence of the NASW's policy on end-of-life decisions? To what extent do you support the client's self-determination in end-of-life decisions?

5. What are your values regarding clients exercising self-determination in the area of making end-of-life decisions? How might your values influence your interventions in such cases?

Values Pertaining to Sexuality

1. What are your values pertaining to sexuality? In what ways might your values in these areas either help or hinder you in making effective contact with clients? Can you think of any areas where you would have a tendency to push clients to make a certain decision with respect to sexual behavior?

2. If you were working with a couple, and if one person had been involved in an extramarital affair for some time, how might this affect your work with them?

Ethical Issues in Counseling Gay and Lesbian Clients

1. How might the values you hold either help or hinder your ability to establish effective relationships with lesbians or gay men?

2. What are the main ethical issues that you think need to be addressed pertaining to counseling gay and lesbian clients?

3. Some writers have suggested that the mental health profession has too often been insensitive to the needs of gay and lesbian clients. What are your thoughts on this matter?

4. Some writers contend that therapists need to find ways to continue to educate themselves about gay identity development. How might you go about educating yourself about resources that are available to gay clients, about affirmative counseling models, and about issues pertaining to gay identity?

5. Do you think that therapists should be ethically required to obtain specialized training in counseling gay and lesbian clients? If yes, what kind of training would you propose? If no, what are your reasons for not requiring this specialized training?

6. From your vantage point, what do you consider to be the special needs of gay and lesbian clients? How might you address these needs in your counseling?

7. For those counselors who believe that homosexuality is immoral, do you think that they have an ethical right to counsel gay or lesbian clients?

CHAPTER 4 — Client Rights and Counselor Responsibilities

Client's Right to Give Informed Consent

1. How is informed consent a basic right of clients?

2. What are some common themes found in the various ethical codes pertaining to informed consent?

3. From a *legal* perspective, what are the three elements involved in adequate informed consent? Define these terms: capacity, comprehension of information, and voluntariness.

4. What are some of your ideas on how you would go about educating clients about informed consent?

5. If you were to create an informed consent document that you would give your clients, what are the main elements that would be contained in this document?

6. Do you think that your clients should have access to their files? Why or why not?

7. Do you think clients have a right to know their diagnostic classification?

The Counselor's Responsibilities in Record Keeping

1. What are the main points of the ethics codes pertaining to keeping records?

2. What is the main purpose of maintaining client records? What should be the general content of these records?

3. Are there any differences between the ethical and legal obligations pertaining to record keeping?

4. What is your stance on record keeping? What kind of records do you think would be most helpful?

Counseling in a Managed Care Environment
1. How did managed care come about?

2. What are some of the key differences between the fee-for-service system of private practice and the newer system of managed care?

3. Identify some of the main advantages and disadvantages of the managed care system, for both the client and the therapist? How can clients best be served given the limited mental-health resources?

4. What are some of the main ethical issues associated with managed care?

Counseling Children and Adolescents
1. What are some laws that you would need to be aware of if you were to work with minors?

2. How might you obtain informed consent of minors? Would you see children or adolescents without parental consent?

3. How might you explain resistance that you may get as you counsel reluctant children and adolescents? What are some possible meanings of this resistance, and how would you work with it?

4. Why is specialized training needed for those who counsel children and adolescents? What kind of training do you think is essential?

Involuntary Commitment and Human Rights
1. Before involuntarily committing a client, what would be some of the steps that you would take? What other courses of action would you take before you resorted to involuntary commitment procedures?

2. What are some of the major ethical and legal issues involved in the process of involuntary commitment?

Malpractice Liability in the Helping Professions

1. How would you define malpractice?

2. What does civil liability mean?

3. What constitutes professional negligence?

4. What is the meaning of the concept of "standard of care"?

5. What four conditions must be present in malpractice litigation? Define these four elements of malpractice: duty, breach of duty, injury, and causation.

6. What are the two main grounds for malpractice suits? [What kind of violations have received the greatest attention in the literature?]

7. Be able to describe each of the following as a cause of malpractice suits:
*   failure to obtain informed consent
*   client abandonment
*   departing from established therapeutic practices
*   practicing beyond the scope of competency
*   misdiagnosis
*   unhealthy transference relationships
*   sexual abuse of a client
*   failure to control a dangerous client
*   managed care and malpractice
*   false memories

8. What has been the impact of malpractice litigation on practitioners?

9. What are some precautions that you would like take in dealing with high-risk clients?

10. What are some ways to protect yourself from malpractice suits? Identify specific safeguards and risk management strategies to lessen the chance of being successfully sued.

11. What course of action might you follow in a malpractice suit?

12. How do legal liability and ethical practice overlap at times?

CHAPTER 5—Confidentiality: Ethical and Legal Aspects

Confidentiality, Privileged Communication, and Privacy
1.   Define these terms: confidentiality, privileged communication, and privacy. How are these related concepts? How is each term distinct?

2.   How does privileged communication differ from confidentiality?

3.   What ethical and legal ramifications of confidentiality would you want to present to your clients? What are the limits of confidentiality?

4.   What limitations do you see on the confidentiality of the therapeutic relationship? When would you feel it necessary that confidentiality be compromised? How might you educate your clients about the purposes and limits of confidentiality?

Duty to Warn and Protect
1.   What is involved in the therapist's duty to protect potential victims from dangerous acts of violent crimes?

2.   What are the major implications of the Tarasoff case?

3.   What was the ruling in the Bradley case?

4.   What are the implications of the legal ruling in the Jablonski case?

5.   What are the implications of the decision in the Hedlund case?

6.   In what ways did the Jaffee case extend the confidentiality privilege?

7.   What might be the consequences of the Jaffee case for licensed therapists and their clients?

8.   How might your therapeutic practices be modified in light of your understanding of the above court cases?

9. What guidelines might you employ for dealing with dangerous clients? How might you go about making the determination of whether or not a person is potentially dangerous to self or others?

10. What are the ethical and legal duties to protect suicidal clients?

11. What are a few guidelines for assessing suicidal behavior?

12. What are the arguments in the case *for* suicide prevention?

13. What are the arguments in the case *against* suicide prevention?

14. What is your stance on the issue of suicide prevention?

Protecting Children From Harm

1. Once you suspect child abuse, what are you expected to do from both an ethical and a legal standpoint? Can you think of situations where what is ethical and what is legal might be in conflict in situations involving child abuse? What would you do if you experienced such a conflict?

2. What are your thoughts about the mandatory reporting laws of suspected cases of child or elder abuse?

3. Some believe that professionals should decide whether or not to report child abuse if their client is an offender, on the grounds that reporting could result in the end of therapy with this client. What do you think?

4. A review of some literature reveals that clinicians are hesitant to report suspected child abuse unless they are fairly certain that abuse is currently occurring. Do you think that ethical practice demands that practitioners report abuse, regardless of how long ago it occurred?

5. How do you distinguish abuse from harsh punishment? What cultural factors might enter into this assessment?

Confidentiality and HIV/AIDS-Related Issues

1. What do you see your ethical responsibilities as being with respect to educating yourself about the problems involved in working with HIV-positive clients and with persons with AIDS?

2. What are some of the common fears and misconceptions associated with HIV and AIDS? As a professional, what responsibilities, if any, do you think you have in educating the public about the disease?

3. What are the ethical issues involved in either maintaining or breaching confidentiality with clients who are HIV-positive and who are sexually active? Do you think you have a duty to warn and to protect identified third parties? What are the legal considerations in these situations?

4. How might an HIV-positive client who refuses to inform his or her partner of his or her status, a matter related to duty to warn and protect?

5. Do Tarasoff principles apply in AIDS-related psychotherapy?

6. What are the ethical implications, if any, involved in dealing with clients who have tested positive for HIV? What rights do your clients have who are HIV-positive? What are the rights of their partners? How do you balance the rights of both parties?

7. What key issues do you think are involved in considering the handling of confidentiality in HIV and AIDS-related therapy cases? What are some of the main ethical and legal considerations in these cases?

8. From an ethical perspective, what kind of special training on HIV-related issues should counselors receive?

CHAPTER 6—Issues in Theory, Practice, and Research

Developing a Counseling Stance
1. How would you describe your counseling stance? What are your assumptions about the nature of counseling and the nature of people?

2. How does your theoretical orientation affect your view of practice? In what way might your theoretical views become an ethical issue?

The Division of Responsibility in Therapy
1. In what way is therapy a joint venture of both the client and the therapist?

2. What are your thoughts on the division of responsibility in the therapeutic relationship?

3. Under what circumstances might this division of responsibility become an ethical concern?

Deciding on the Goals of Counseling

1. What do you consider to be a few of the most important goals of counseling?

2. Who is in the best position to determine therapeutic goals?

3. In what way might the process of deciding on goals for therapy become an ethical issue?

Diagnosis as a Professional Issue

1. What is the main purpose of the diagnostic approach?

2. What does differential diagnosis mean?

3. What are the main arguments *for* psychodiagnosis?

4. What are the main arguments *against* psychodiagnosis?

5. What are some potential ethical issues associated with the process of diagnosis?

6. If you worked in an agency that required you to formulate a diagnosis and a treatment plan based upon this diagnosis at the initial session, how would this influence your practice?

7. What is the role of a client's ethnic and cultural background as it pertains to the process of diagnosis?

8. What is your position on psychodiagnosis?

9. What are some possible ethical issues surrounding diagnostic practices? Can you think of any unethical diagnostic practices?

Using Tests in Counseling

1. What guidelines would help you decide when you might want to use tests for counseling purposes?

2. What are some main *ethical* considerations in using tests?

3. In interpreting test results to a client, how would you take into consideration his or her ethnicity and cultural background?

4. What are some multicultural considerations in using tests?

The Use of Techniques in Counseling and Therapy

1. What are the main *ethical* issues regarding the appropriate and ethical use of techniques?

2. In what situations is it likely that techniques could be abused?

3. What are the ethical issues involved in adapting techniques to the needs of the client?

4. What are your guidelines for using techniques in an ethical way?

Ethical Issues in Psychotherapeutic Research

1. How is informed consent an ethical issue in research?

2. Do you think that it is ever justified to use deception in psychological research?

3. What are some potential ethical issues involved in situations involving withholding of treatment for experimental purposes?

4. Some writers have criticized the ethical codes of both ACA and APA on the grounds that they are not responsive and relevant to the pragmatic research needs of minorities. What are your thoughts on this topic?

CHAPTER 7 Managing Boundaries and Multiple Relationships

Dual/Multiple Relationships in Perspective

1. What is the definition of dual or multiple relationships? What are some of the more common forms of dual/multiple relationship?

2. Some writers focus on the problems inherent in dual/multiple relationships. Mention some of these problems that are associated with dual/multiple relationships.

3. Are all dual/multiple relationships necessarily unethical? Why or why not?

4. Some claim that dual or multiple relationships are inherent in the work of all helping professions, that they are not necessarily harmful, and that there may be some beneficial aspects to some dual relationships. What do you think of this perspective?

5. Some hold that dual/multiple relationships are inevitable and unavoidable, and that it is the responsibility of the professional to find ways to monitor the risks and safeguard clients. What are your reactions to this view?

6. What are the reasons that dual/multiple relationships are generally prohibited?

7. What are some issues to consider and factors involved in determining the degree to which dual/multiple relationships pose problems or raise the potential for harm to clients?

8. Dr. Arnold Lazarus takes the position that certain boundaries and ethics actually diminish therapeutic effectiveness. He believes that some well-intentioned guidelines can backfire and that rather than being driven by rules that it is best for therapists to engage in a process of negotiation in many multiple relationships. What do you think about his views?

Bartering for Professional Services

1. What do the ethics codes state about bartering?

41

2.   When is bartering problematic? Why do some contend that bartering of services and goods for therapy services raises ethical concerns? What cultural factors need to be taken into account in determining whether to barter?

3. What are some arguments both for and against the practice of bartering for therapeutic services?

4.   If a client were unable to pay for your services, would you be inclined to consider bartering if the client initiated this as a solution? If yes, what guidelines would you want to establish between you and your client? If you would not be willing to engage in bartering, what alternatives, if any, might you suggest?

Social Relationships with Clients

1.   What are the potential problems in situations where there is a blending of both personal and professional relationships? Do social relationships of any form necessarily interfere with therapeutic relationships?

2.   When do you think that social relationships with *current* clients are unethical? What about the ethics of forming personal or social relationships with *former* clients?

3.   Some counselors take the position that counseling and friendship should not be mixed. The argument is that blending social relationships with professional ones simultaneously can negatively affect the therapy process, the friendship, or both. What are your ideas about this viewpoint?

4.   Some peer counselors might claim that friendships before or during counseling are actually positive factors in establishing trust and a productive therapeutic relationship. What do you think?

Sexual Attraction in the Client/Therapist Relationship

1.   What are your thoughts on the matter of sexual attractions in the client/therapist relationship? To what extent have you thought about or discussed this topic?

2. If a client were attracted to you and expressed this, what do you think you would do? What if you were attracted to a client? What might you do or say?

3. What kind of education and training do you think graduate programs should include for trainees on the matter of learning how to deal effectively with sexual attractions?

4. If you were designing a training program to help counselor trainees learn how to recognize and effectively deal with sexual attractions in therapy, what would your program look like?

Sexual Relationships: Legal and Ethical Issues

1. What are the arguments for and against the use of touching in therapy?

2. Under what practices does touching tend to lead to intercourse in the therapy relationship?

3. What do the studies show concerning the frequency of sexual contact with clients?

4. What do the ethical standards say about sexual intimacy in the therapeutic relationship?

5. What are the reasons that sexual intimacy between therapist and client is considered unethical and unprofessional?

6. What are some common misconceptions that tend to influence the therapist's decision to engage in sexual intimacies with a client?

7. What do the studies reveal about the harmful effects of sexual intimacy on clients?

8. What are some legal sanctions against sexual violators? What are some ethical sanctions?

9. What are some of the major reasons that clients who have been victims of sexual misconduct by a therapist are slow to report the matter to the proper authorities?

10. What are the ethical and legal aspects of therapists forming either social or romantic relationships with former clients? What specific factors need to be addressed by therapists before they get involved in any personal way with former clients?

11. Under what circumstances might you be inclined to report unethical behavior of a colleague?

12. What do the studies show pertaining to graduate students in psychology and their willingness to report unethical behaviors?

CHAPTER 8—Professional Competence and Training Issues

Therapist Competence

1. What are your thoughts on how you could determine your own level of competence?

2. How might you know when to refer a client because of limited competence? In such a case, how would you go about making this referral? What would you do if a client refused to accept your referral?

3. What are a few ethical issues in the training of therapists?

4. What are your thoughts about the assumption that training programs need to be designed so that students can learn a good deal more about themselves as well as acquire theoretical knowledge?

5. If you were a part of a screening committee to determine which candidates would be admitted to a counselor-training program, how would you best go about assessing a candidate's personal characteristics? What other factors would you want to use in screening applicants for a counselor-preparation program?

6. What do you think should be taught in preparing counselors for practice?

7. How do you think practitioners can best be trained? What are your thoughts on the training of therapists?

8.   What should the criteria be for graduating from a graduate program in counseling? How can the evaluation process of trainees best be handled?

Professional Licensing and Credentialing

1.   Define the following terms: registration, licensure, certification

2.   Does professional licensing indicate professional competence? Give reasons for your answer.

3.   What are the purposes of legislative regulation of professional practice?

4.   What are the arguments for and against professional licensing and credentialing?

5.   The process of licensure, certification, credentialing, and registration can promote a sense of professional identity. It can also lead to professional jealousy over turf battles and interprofessional bickering. What are your views on the process of regulation of professional practice?

Specialties within the Counseling Profession

1.   Identify some of the main specialties within the counseling profession. What are some of the advantages of specializations? Any disadvantages?

2.   Do training programs have a responsibility to produce competent generalists as well as specialists? Should one be a generalist before becoming a specialist?

Continuing Education and Demonstration of Competence

1 .   What are your views on continuing education as a way to maintain competence? Are you in favor of *requiring* continuing education as a condition for relicensure?

2 .   How can peer review be a means of ensuring quality?

3.   What value do peer-consultation groups have for counselors-in-training? for experienced practitioners?

CHAPTER 9—Issues in Supervision and Consultation

Ethical and Legal Issues in Clinical Supervision

1. In what ways are supervisors responsible for the actions of their trainees?

2. What are the main roles and responsibilities that counseling supervisors have toward supervisees?

3. Because supervisors are expected to be knowledgeable regarding ethical, legal, and regulatory aspects of the profession, what kind of special training do you think supervisors need to function effectively?

4. Which do you consider to be the proper focus of the supervision process—the client or the counselor?

5. What is the role of informed consent in the supervision process?

6. Some consider negligent supervision to be fertile grounds for malpractice action. From your perspective, what constitutes negligence in supervision?

7. What are some other legal aspects pertaining to supervision? What is the difference between direct liability and vicarious liability?

Competence in Supervision

1. From both an ethical and a legal perspective, why is competence a main element in supervision? What kinds of experiences do supervisors need to be competent? Does possession of an advanced degree imply that a counselor can also supervise effectively?

2. What kind of understanding of racial and ethnic diversity issues is essential for supervisors? What are some of the main issues regarding multicultural supervision?

Multiple Roles and Relationships in the Supervisory Process

1. Why are dual or multiple relationships in the supervision process an ethical issue? What are some examples of such relationships that you think are most problematic?

46

2. Sexual intimacies between supervisors and supervisees pose several problems. What problems can you think of in such situations?

3. What are your thoughts about supervisors who combine supervision with personal counseling, especially in cases where a supervisee's personal problems are interfering with providing effective counseling?

4. What are the ethics involved of educators who counsel their *current* students? What about educators or supervisors who eventually accept a *former* student or supervisee as a client in therapy?

Ethical and Professional Issues in Consultation

1. How is consultation defined? What are the targets of the consultation process? What are the aims of the consultation process?

2. Why is a code of ethics needed for consultants?

3. What are some of the important ethical principles for consultants?

4. What are some unique dual relationship problems confronting consultants?

5. What kind of training do you think consultants need to function competently?

6. What are some examples of dual relationships in the consulting process? In what way can these relationships be problematic for both the consultee and the consultant?

7. From an ethical standpoint, what do you think consultants should know about an organization before they agree to enter into a contract with a particular group?

8. How are hidden agendas a particular problem in the practice of consulting?

9. If a consultant were to discover that the members of a particular organization were in need of personal therapy, what do you think is the consultant's responsibility?

47

10. How is consultation with colleagues a good practice throughout one's professional career?

CHAPTER 10—Multicultural Perspectives and Diversity Issues

The Need for a Multicultural Emphasis

1. Define each of the following terms: ethnicity, culture, minority group, multicultural, culturally encapsulated counselor, ethnic-sensitive practices, racism, and stereotypes.

2. How is cultural tunnel vision sometimes a problem with mental health practitioners?

3. What are some steps you can take to deal effectively with cultural diversity and pluralism?

4. What are some reasons you can offer for the need for a multicultural emphasis in the practice of counseling?

Ethical Codes in Multicultural Counseling

1. What are the limitations of existing codes for multicultural counseling?

2. To what degree, if at all, are the ACA *Code of Ethics and Standards of Practice* and the APA *Ethical Principles* culturally encapsulated? What evidence is there in these codes that they are culturally sensitive?

3. What evidence is there that the NASW's *Code of Ethics* deals with diversity perspectives and multicultural concerns?

Cultural Values and Assumptions in Therapy

1. What are some of the main differences between Western and Eastern values? What are the implications of these differences for practice?

2. In what senses are contemporary theories of therapy and therapeutic practices grounded in Western assumptions?

3. What are some specific values associated with a Western orientation?

4.   What are some specific values associated with an Eastern orientation?

5.   What are some common stereotypical beliefs held by some counselors regarding minority clients?

6.   How are a counselor's assumptions about self-disclosure pertinent in counseling certain ethnic groups? How about the counselor's assumptions about assertiveness? About self actualization? About nonverbal behavior? About directness? About trusting?

Matching Client and Counselor

1.   What are some factors that have a bearing on the question "Does a counselor have to share the racial and cultural backgrounds of the client to be effective?"

2.   What are your thoughts on the issue of matching client and counselor? In what areas do you think it is important to be matched with your client? How can you bridge any differences?

3.   What is the basic difference between an intentional racist and an unintentional racist? In what way might you be an unintentional racist? What are some of the best ways of changing any unintentional racist attitudes or behaviors?

Multicultural Training for Counselors

1.   Becoming a culturally aware therapist is not an either/or condition, but it is best considered on a continuum from being unaware of cultural issues to a heightened awareness of the role that cultural factors play in counseling. Where do you see yourself on this continuum? How aware are you of the cultural dynamics that enter into a therapeutic relationship? How comfortable do you feel in working with cultural differences that may emerge in helping relationships?

2.   What are the main characteristics of the culturally skilled counselor?

3.   What do you consider to be the essential components of multicultural counseling? Include a discussion of beliefs and attitudes, knowledge, and skills of culturally skilled counselors.

4.   What are your thoughts on an ideal training program for multicultural counseling?

CHAPTER 11—The Counselor in the Community

The Community Mental-Health Orientation
1.   What are some of the main ethical responsibilities you have to the community and to society?

2.   What are the four main activities that make up a comprehensive community-counseling program?

3.   How does the community mental-health approach differ from the traditional approach to therapy?

4.   Within the community perspective, what is the professional's role in educating the community?

5.   What is the community worker's responsibility in the area of influencing policymakers?

6.   What are the main goals of the outreach approach? What are some strategies of this approach?

7.   What is the meaning of being an advocate for clients? What are some examples of counselors assuming the role of client advocate?

8.   Describe each of the following alternative roles counselors might play in working in the community: change agent, consultant, adviser, advocate, facilitator of indigenous support system, and facilitator of indigenous healing system.

The Use of Paraprofessionals
1.   What is the reason for the increasing use of paraprofessionals?

2.   What are the types of paraprofessionals involved in human services?

3.   What are some training standards that are needed for paraprofessionals?

4.   What implications does the trend toward the use of paraprofessionals have upon the roles professionals will assume?

Working within a System

1.   How do you think you could retain a sense of vitality and integrity, while working within the boundaries of a system? How does this become an ethical issue?

2.   What do you see as your relationship as a counselor to the agency where you work?

3.   What are some ways that you can deal with the tendency to avoid responsibility by blaming the institution or system where you work?

4.   What strategies can you think of for not getting lost in the system, yet for attaining your own professional goals? How might you assume power within the system?

CHAPTER 12—Ethical Issues in Marital and Family Therapy

Ethical Standards in Marital and Family Therapy

1.   What are some ethical standards that are specific to the practice of marital and family therapy?

2.   What are a few key ethical problems that face family therapists?

Contemporary Professional Issues

1.   What are the major personal characteristics needed for an effective family therapist?

2.   What are the educational requirements of marital and family therapists, according to the AAMFT?

3.   What are the main standards of training and clinical experience?

4.   What is the rationale for expecting family therapists to experience their own personal therapy and to work with their family of origin?

Values in Marital and Family Therapy

1. In what ways do the therapist's values take on special significance in counseling couples and families?

2. What are some areas where you might have difficulty in counseling families because of your values?

Gender-Sensitive Marital and Family Therapy

1. How are sex-role stereotypes a special concern for therapists who work with couples and families? How might your own values pertaining to traditional and nontraditional family arrangements influence your practice with couples and families?

2. How are gender stereotypes problematic in counseling both men and women?

3. When do the gender stereotypes of counselors become an ethical issue?

4. What are some ways of becoming a nonsexist family therapist? How can you use the therapeutic process to challenge the oppressive consequences of stereotyped roles and expectations in the family?

5. What are your thoughts on what constitutes gender-aware therapy?

Responsibilities of Marital and Family Therapists

1. What are some special responsibilities of marital and family therapists?

2. When is it necessary to consult in this area of therapy?

Confidentiality and Informed Consent in Marital and Family Therapy

1. How is confidentiality a special issue in marital and family therapy? What are some issues pertaining to confidentiality that a family therapist needs to clarify from the outset with each family member? What problems might you have in this area if you were to work with a family?

2. How is informed consent a special consideration in marital and family therapy?

3. What are some issues involved in cases where therapists require attendance by all the members of a family as a condition for family therapy?

4. What are your thoughts about conducting a family therapy session without all the members of the family being present?

CHAPTER 13—Ethical Issues in Group Work

Training and Supervision of Group Leaders

1. What are some kinds of knowledge and skills you think are essential for effective group counselors? What about supervised experience in group work?

2. What are some of the main provisions of the *Professional Standards for the Training of Group Workers*? What do you think about different standards of training for the various group work specialties?

3. What kind of training program in group counseling would you like to participate in? What can you do to get the training in group work you are likely to need?

Co-Leadership

1. Ethically, when would you feel ready to lead or to co-lead a group in a community agency?

2. What ethical issues can you identify as they relate to co-leadership practices? Mention some advantages and disadvantages of the co-leadership model?

3. What qualities would you look for in selecting a co-leader?

Ethical Issues in Group Membership

1. In recruiting members for a group, what would you want to tell members before they made the decision to join a group?

2. What are some ethical issues involved in screening and selecting group members? How do you decide whom to include and exclude? Are there any ethical alternatives when screening is not practical or possible?

3.   What kind of preparation and orientation would you want to provide for members in a group you would lead?

4.   Should group membership always be voluntary? Are there any situations in which it is ethical to require participation in a group?

5.   Once members make a commitment to be a part of a group, do they have the right to leave at any time they choose?

6.   What are a few of the major psychological risks in group participation? What could you do to minimize these risks?

Confidentiality in Groups

1.   What are the main ethical, legal, and professional issues pertaining to confidentiality in group situations?

2.   As a group leader, how would you teach your members about confidentiality? How would you encourage confidentiality?

3.   When, and under what circumstances, would you breach confidentiality in a group?

Values in Group Counseling

1.   How can a group leader's values influence the group process? What is the ethical way a leader can use his or her values without imposing them on members?

2.   What ethical issues are involved in members pressuring other members to adopt a particular value stance or to make a decision of how to live?

Uses and Abuses of Group Techniques

1.   What are some guidelines to avoid abusing techniques in a group?

2.   How is therapist competence an ethical issue as it pertains to using group techniques?

3.   What are some ethical concerns pertaining to using group techniques with culturally diverse client populations?

The Consultation and Referral Process

1.   What are some ethical guidelines pertaining to the consultation and referral process as it pertains to group work? In what cases would you seek consultation in your work as a group leader?

2.   When might you make a referral of a member to another professional?

3.   What responsibilities do leaders have in suggesting ways members might continue engaging in personal change once they have completed a group? What kind of knowledge about resources is needed?

Issues Concerning Termination

1.   What ethical and practical issues would you be concerned with as a group moves toward termination?

2.   What kind of follow-up might you design for a group you have led?

CHAPTER QUIZZES for
Issues and Ethics in the Helping Professions, Fifth Edition

Directions: The questions below are divided into the following three areas.

1. Fact (F), referring to a questions that pertain to definitional or objective information.

2. Conceptual (C), in which the question is based on information generalized from particular instances and requires the student to interpret their responses.

3. Applied (A), based on case studies in which the response tests for the student's ability to apply theory to practical instances.

The alphabetical letter is followed by the page number in which the test question was derived. (Only the first page number is used where two pages were needed to comprise the question.)

Test Questions for Chapter 1

INTRODUCTION TO PROFESSIONAL ETHICS

F-3   1.   _____ is concerned with perspectives of right and proper conduct and involves an evaluation of actions on the basis of some broader cultural context or religious standard.

       a.   Ethical conduct

       b.   Community standards

    *c.   Morality

       d.   Professionalism

A-3   2.   Robert runs into the office, unprepared and frustrated because he is late for his weekly appointment with his first client of the day. He is consistently late for his appointments and his behavior is

a.   immoral.

b.   illegal.

c.   unethical.

*d.   unprofessional.

A-4   3.   James and Mary were going to counseling for marital problems and the counselor decided to meet each partner in an individual session before meeting them as a couple. James confided that he was HIV-positive and was not going to tell his spouse because she would know that he had been unfaithful. The counselor decided to break confidentially after attempts to encourage James to inform his wife of his condition. The counselor's action

a.   was illegal and may result in sanctions.

*b.   may be considered ethical, yet the practitioner could be in violation of a legal standard.

c.   was unethical since confidentiality was broken.

d.   was ethical and meets the American Counseling Association standard regarding contagious diseases which states that practitioners must report when a client is HIV positive.

A-5   4.   Elizabeth is a beginning practitioner and is counseling in a manner where she merely acts in compliance with the law and follows minimal ethical standards. She is at the first level of ethical functioning which is

a.   personal ethics.

b.   aspiration ethics.

*c.   mandatory ethics.

d.   basic ethics.

C-8   5.   The basic purpose of professional code of ethics is to

   *a.   educate professionals about sound ethical conduct, provide a mechanism for professional accountability, and serve as a catalyst for improving practice.

   b.   protect professionals from lawsuits.

   c.   set standards that will be understood and enforced across all cultures.

   d.   ensure that standards remain consistent over time.

A-9   6.   A formal complaint was filed against Harry for sexually harassing a female client. This is not the first complaint against him and he was previously warned that a major sanction would be imposed if he continued his unethical actions. The professional ethics committee to which he belongs recommended that Harry

   a.   be on probation during his entire career.

   b.   resign from his job.

   c.   work without supervision on his word that he will not harass any client again.

   *d.   be expelled from the organization.

C-10   7.   The counselor who asks the questions "Am I doing what is best for my client?" rather than "Is this situation unethical?" is functioning from the following ethical perspective.

   a.   principle ethics

   *b.   virtue ethics

   c.   value ethics

   d.   practical ethics

C-10   8.   The virtuous professional

     a. is motivated to do what is right because he/she feels obligated.

     b. functions within his/her professional code of ethics because he/she fears the consequences if he/she does not.

    *c. possesses vision and discernment, which involves sensitivity, judgment, and understanding, and leads to decisive ethical actions.

     d. typically focuses on moral issues with the goals of solving a particular dilemma.

A-10   9.   Richard is counseling a male Asian client and is encouraging him to go away to college even though he is expected to take care of his aging parents. Richard is violating the following basic moral principle in making ethical decisions.

    *a. nonmaleficence

     b. autonomy

     c. beneficence

     d. fidelity

A-13   10.   Jan is an incest victim and is covered for six sessions by insurance. Her counselor is in private practice and knows that Jan needs more sessions. She decides to offer Jan her services pro bono. In making the ethical decision to ensure that her client has equal access to services, the counselor is using the basic moral principal of

     a. fidelity.

    *b. justice.

     c. beneficence.

     d. veracity.

Test Questions for Chapter 2

THE COUNSELOR AS A PERSON AND AS A PROFESSIONAL

A-35   1.   Rhonda is a counselor at a drug and alcohol treatment center. She grew up in an alcoholic home and is not fully aware of the "unfinished business" she has with her parents. She is still angry and resentful with her parents for growing up in an alcoholic family system. It is most likely that Rhonda will

       a.   be able to understand her addicted clients through her own childhood experiences.

       b.   examine her unresolved conflicts as she continues to work in the treatment center.

     *c.   obstruct the progress of her clients as they attempt to move toward recovery.

       d.   feel comfortable with her clients because she is familiar with their behavior.

C-39   2.   Ronald directs his clients toward solutions instead of encouraging them to seek alternatives for themselves. He is likely to have a strong need

       a.   for approval.

     *b.   to feel a sense of achievement and accomplishment.

       c.   to empower his client.

       d.   to nurture his client.

C-37   3.   Counselors who have unresolved personal conflicts

     *a.   need to recognize that their problems may interfere with their effectiveness and refrain from activities that would harm a client.

       b.   must resolve all their difficulties before counseling others.

       c.   are quite effective because they know how difficult it is to resolve problems.

       d.   need to repress anxiety-provoking issues in their own lives before becoming effective counselors.

F-45   4.   _____ is the process whereby clients place past feelings or attitudes they had toward significant people in their lives onto their therapist.

*a.   Transference

b.   Countertransference

c.   Projection

d.   Mirroring

A-45   5.   Becky believes that her counselor is an expert, all-knowing and all-powerful. She is exhibiting the following transference pattern as she views her counselor as a

a.   nurturer.

b.   mentor.

*c.   seer.

d.   wizard.

C-48   6.   Countertransference can be constructive in the therapeutic relationship when the therapist

a.   is overprotective with the client.

b.   treats clients in benign ways.

*c.   recognizes transference patterns and can help the client change old dysfunctional themes.

d.   over identifies with the client's problems.

A-48   7.   Joanne finds herself wanting to solve her client's problems which are similar to the issues her daughter is going through. Joanne gives advice and feels frustrated when her client won't follow through on her suggestions. Her emotional reactions to her client, which involve her own projections is based on

a.   transference.

b.   nurturance.

*c.   countertransference.

d.   caretaking.

C-48   8.   When counselors become overly concerned with meeting their own needs or pushing their own personal agendas, their behavior becomes

     a.   annoying to the client.

    *b.   unethical.

     c.   illegal.

     d.   narcissistic.

C-51   9.   Sexual or romantic feelings toward a client

     a.   are the result of seductive behavior on the part of the client and needs to be ignored.

     b.   are an indicator that the client needs to be referred to another counselor.

     c.   are unethical, counter therapeutic, and also illegal in many states.

    *d.   does not necessarily mean that the counselor cannot effectively work with the client.

     e.   never occurs if the counselor is operating within their professional code of ethics.

C-59   10.   Deutsch and Farber found surprisingly similar results in their surveys of therapists' perceptions of stressful client behavior. In both studies therapists reported that the following clients' behavior was *most* stressful for them.

     a.   aggression and hostility

    *b.   suicidal statements

     c.   severely depressed clients

     d.   premature termination of therapy

     e.   agitated anxiety

VALUES AND THE HELPING RELATIONSHIP

C-68   1.   In regards to values in the counseling process, the authors contend that

   *a.   it is incumbent that counselors clarify their values and the ways in which they enter the therapeutic process.

   b.   counselors can avoid communicating values to their clients by not explicitly sharing them.

   c.   it is best to keep values hidden so they won't contaminate their client's choices.

   d.   it is a counselor's job to help clients conform to socially acceptable standards.

C-78   2.   A cross-cultural counselor who perceives reality exclusively through the filters of his or her own life experiences is said to be culturally

   a.   immersed.

   b.   ignorant.

   *c.   blind or encapsulated.

   d.   biased.

A-83   3.   Mary is seeking abortion counseling from a practitioner who has been actively involved in the pro-life movement. The therapist has extreme discomfort with Mary's values and doesn't think he could maintain objectivity. It would be best if he

   a.   doesn't share his values with Mary and work within the value system of his clients.

   b.   help Mary to understand his values so she can make a different decision concerning her pregnancy.

   *c.   refers Mary to a therapist who shares the client's values.

   d.   set firm boundaries with Mary on what she can discuss in regards to her pregnancy.

A-78 4. An Asian-American pre-med college student is seeking counseling on campus. He appears to be excessively concerned with failing his parent's expectations since he harbors wishes about becoming a social worker and knows that his parents would disapprove. The counselor attempts to force him to share his negative feelings with his parents. In this case, the counselor is operating from an assumption that is

    a. culturally focused.

*b. culturally encapsulated.

    c. culturally challenging.

    d. culturally aware.

F-82 5. _____ refers to a personal inclination or desire for a relationship with the transcendent or God.

    a. Religion

*b. Spirituality

    c. Faith

    d. Belief

C-63 6. The following is true regarding spiritual and religious values in counseling:

    a. Clients can gain insight into the ways that most religious beliefs and values are the reason for their shame, guilt and anxiety.

*b. Clients may discover that what they are doing is based on beliefs that are no longer functional.

    c. Spiritual counseling encourages the client to turn their problems over to God and not take any action themselves.

    d. Religious themes need to be addressed in every counseling session.

A-85   7.   Ruth is counseling with a woman who describes an extremely unhappy marriage. Ruth suggests that she consider leaving her husband. The client has a deep spiritual conviction that marriage is for life and is not willing to consider divorce as an option. Ruth attempts to change her client's viewpoint as being unhealthy. In this case, Ruth is

   a.   teaching her client to look at the negative consequences of her decision.

   b.   exploring the client's spiritual reasons for staying in the marriage.

   *c. imposing her values on the client instead of exploring the client's reasons for staying in the marriage.

   d.   helping her client to explore healthy options.

A-91   8.   Thomas has full-blown AIDS and has decided to end his life rather than continue to suffer. The counselor he is working with does not condone rational suicide. In this case, the counselor needs to

   *a. refer him to a competent professional qualified to assist the client.

   b.   learn as much as possible about the course of the client's illness.

   c.   explore the impact of the client's religious beliefs on making his decision to end his life.

   d.   help the client seek medical treatment that will help him cope with his pain.

C-93   9.   According to the National Association of Social Workers policy on working with end-of-life decisions, it would *not* be appropriate for the professional to

   a.   facilitate exploration of alternatives.

   b.   help patients express their thoughts and feelings.

   *c. deliver, supply, or personally participate in the commission of an act of assisted suicide.

   d.   provide information to make an informed choice.

   e.   deal with issues of grief and loss.

A-101 10. Marie is working with a lesbian client who is in a dysfunctional relationship with another woman. She is seeking counseling to sort out her options regarding leaving her emotionally abusive partner. Marie can assist her client by

    a. automatically attributing her client's problems to her sexual orientation.

    b. attempting to change the sexual orientation of her client.

   *c. supporting her client's attempt to leave the abusive relationship, work on her abuse issues, and eventually enter into a positive lesbian relationship.

    d. encouraging her client to realize how difficult it is to live in a lesbian relationship.

Test Questions for Chapter 4

CLIENT RIGHTS AND COUNSELOR RESPONSIBILITIES

C-112 1. Informed consent generally implies that the person

    a. does not have the capacity to consent.

    b. verbally gives consent.

    c. has been persuaded or coerced to sign the consent form.

   *d. has the capacity to consent and has freely, without undue influence expressed consent.

F-114 2. _____ to give informed consent means that the client has the ability to make rational decisions.

    a. Comprehension of information

    b. Voluntariness

   *c. Capacity

    d. Willingness

C-117   3.   Written consent forms should *not* include

     a.   a discussion of how a managed care system will affect the treatment, if applicable.

    *b.   a detailed description of what will occur in therapy and a guarantee that the client will resolve their issues.

     c.   a statement describing the counselor's theoretical orientation and how this will affect treatment.

     d.   clarification pertaining to fees and charges and procedures for filing for insurance reimbursement.

C-120   4.   John is seeking counseling through his managed care provider and he needs to be informed that

    *a.   a financial incentive exists to limit the amount or type of service provided.

     b.   he has the right to expect unlimited sessions.

     c.   his insurance provider will not have access to his records.

     d.   no referrals will be made upon termination of therapy.

C-123   5.   Most ethical codes specify that therapist should

     a.   be available to their clients even when they are on vacation.

     b.   inform clients that their records are inaccessible to them.

    *c.   inform clients that a diagnosis can become a permanent part of their file and have ramifications in terms of cost of insurance, long-term insurability, and employment.

     d.   alter case notes that are damaging to the client if they are subpoenaed into court.

F-126   6.   _____ should include a record of client and therapist behavior that is clinically relevant, including interventions used, client responses to treatment strategies, the evolving treatment plan, and any follow-up measures taken.

     a.   Assessments

    *b.   Progress notes

     c.   Intakes

     d.   Screenings

C-129   7.   The managed care model,

     a.   allows practitioners to decide what clients need, how and when to treat them, and how long therapy will last.

   *b.   stresses time-limited interventions, cost-effective methods, and a focus on preventative strategies.

     c.   has grown out of demands by practitioners for quality control and stabilizing escalating costs of mental-health care.

     d.   encourages curative interventions, accurate diagnosis and hospital admissions when needed.

     e.   assumes that practitioners will set therapeutic goals of personal growth and self-actualization for their clients.

A-133   8.   Angela is sixteen-years-old and is seeking counseling about birth control since she is having sex without protection and afraid to get pregnant. In most states

   *a.   parental consent is legally required before she can seek help from a therapist.

     b.   she will be referred to a minister for counseling.

     c.   her boyfriend will be arrested for having sex with a minor.

     d.   she has the right to seek counseling about birth control without parental consent.

     e.   she will be given an AIDS test.

A-133   9.   Marie is a counselor who has been working with the parents of their six-year-old daughter. They want Marie to counsel with their child since the effects of their stormy marriage is negatively affecting her behavior. Marie is hesitant to do so since she has no experience working with children. The ethical codes of most professional organizations would specify that

     a.   she would have to use different types of therapy to work effectively with the child.

   *b.   it would be unethical for Marie to counsel the child if she has not been trained in that area.

     c.   she needs to take specialized training in parent education before working with the child.

     d.   Child Protective Services need to be called.

C-137 10. The social policy of de-institutionalization, as it applies to mental-health practices, involves the "least restrictive alternative" which requires that

    a. voluntary commitment be sought only after less restrictive alternatives have failed.

    b. professionals commit clients who are delusional.

    c. practitioners protect themselves from liability by getting a lawyer.

    *d. treatment be no more harsh, hazardous, or intrusive than necessary to achieve therapeutic aims and protect clients and others from physical harm.

F-139 11. _____ is the failure to render professional services or to exercise the degree of skills that is ordinarily expected of other professionals in a similar situation.

    a. Professional negligence

    b. Ethical incompetence

    *c. Malpractice

    d. Malfeasance

C-140 12. Malpractice is generally limited to incidents in which the practitioner

    a. used a procedure within the realm of accepted professional practice.

    *b. employed a technique that he or she was not trained to use.

    c. used a procedure in which the client did not responded favorably.

    d. explained the possible consequences of treatment and the client still wanted to participate in the process.

C-140 13. To succeed in a malpractice claim, the plaintiff needs to show that a breach of duty did exist in which

    a. the practitioner failed to foresee a client's intention to harm themselves even after a comprehensive risk assessment was made.

    b. the client failed to get better in spite of reasonable care.

    c. there was no professional relationship between therapist and client.

    *d. the practitioner failed to provide the appropriate standard of care.

C-141 14. _____ have received the greatest attention in the literature as grounds for malpractice suits.

    *a. Violations of confidentiality and sexual misconduct

    b. Client abandonment and misdiagnosis

    c. Failure to obtain informed consent and practicing beyond the scope of competency

    d. Client abandonment and repressed or false memory

A-142 15. Joyce was hospitalized as a result of an attempted suicide. She had tried to call her therapist before taking an overdose of pills, but he could not be reached because he was on vacation and did not provide a substitute while he was gone. This action constitutes the following type of professional negligence.

    a. misdiagnosis

    *b. client abandonment

    c. marked departure from established therapeutic practice

    d. practicing beyond the scope of competency

71

C-143 16. Inappropriate socialization with clients, burdening clients with a counselor's personal problems, and putting clients in awkward business situations are examples of

    a. inappropriate crisis intervention.

    b. established therapeutic practices.

    *c. mishandling of a client's transference or counselor's countertransference.

    d. seeking balance in the counseling relationship.

C-145 17. Two core issues of malpractice as they specifically apply to managed care are

    a. misdiagnosis and client abandonment.

    b. failure to request additional service from the plan or make appropriate referrals when needed.

    c. breach of confidentiality and failure to render crisis intervention.

    *d. standard of care and therapist liability.

C-146 18. The following is a safeguard against malpractice accusations:

    a. Give free sessions until the client is able to pay.

    b. Never engage in bartering under any circumstances.

    c. Avoid client's perception of abandonment by not taking time off.

    *d. Practice in specific areas where you are competent.

C-149 19. In the event that a practitioner is sued he or she should

    a. try to resolve the matter directly with the client.

    b. destroy or alter files or reports that may be incriminating.

    c. discuss the case with other professionals.

    *d. promptly retain an attorney.

F-150 20. _____ can best be viewed as an ongoing process aimed at increasing the range of choices and theresponsibility of the client as an active therapeutic partner.

    a. Diagnosis

  *b. Informed consent

    c. Documentation

    d. Case consultations

Test Questions for Chapter 5

CONFIDENTIALITY: ETHICAL AND LEGAL ISSUES

C-155 1. The central right of clients concerning confidentiality is that

  *a. it guarantees that disclosures during therapy will be protected unless certain legal circumstances are present.

    b. everything said in therapy will always remain confidential.

    c. it is illegal to share information with anyone at anytime unless the client has signed an informed consent.

    d. their records cannot be subpoenaed into court.

A-156 2. James is in court facing drug-related charges and his therapist was subpoenaed to testify in court regarding any discriminating evidence concerning the case. His therapist came to court but refused to answer questions regarding the case or produce James's records. The therapist used the following legal concept to protect himself from forced disclosure:

    a. confidentiality

  *b. privileged communication

    c. client privacy

    d. taking the 5th amendment

F-158 3. _____ as a matter of law, refers to the constitutional right of an individual to decide the time, place, manner, and extent of sharing oneself with others.

    a. Self-disclosure

    b. Privileged communication

  *c. Privacy

    d. Confidentiality

C-161 4. It is illegal and unethical for a therapist to disclose confidential information when

    a. the client consents to disclosure.

    b. there is a duty to warn or to protect third parties.

    c. an emergency exists.

  *d. an employer requests disclosure to determine the mental status of an employee without their consent.

    e. there is a need to obtain appropriate consultations.

C-161 5. Ethical guidelines regarding confidentiality requires that counselors do *not*

    a. allow clerical assistants to handle confidential information.

    b. use client records to consult with experts or peers.

    c. use client case studies to teach or write books even when their clients' identities are disguised.

  *d. disclose client information unless there is clear and imminent danger to client or others or when legal requirements demand that confidential information be revealed.

A-165 6. Susan is quite distressed after finding out that her husband has been unfaithful and tells her counselor that she is so angry that she feels like killing him. In this case, the counselor needs to

   *a. question Susan to determine whether she is likely to do physical harm to her husband.

   b. warn the husband that he is in potential danger.

   c. commit Susan to a hospital until she can overcome her anger.

   d. warn Susan that she can be arrested for making threats against her husband.

C-167 7. The California court's ruling that requires that therapists breach confidentiality in cases where the general welfare and safety of others is involved is a result of the

   a. Bradley Center v. Wessner decision.

   b. Jablonski v. United States decision.

   *c. Tarasoff decision.

   d. Hedlund v. Superior Court decision.

A-167 8. A patient who was extremely upset over his wife's extramarital affair was voluntarily admitted to a psychiatric facility. After repeatedly threatening to kill both of them and admitting to his therapist that he had a weapon, he was given a weekend pass to visit his children who were living with his wife. He met his wife and lover at the house and killed both of them. The Bradley case illustrates the duty

   *a. not to negligently release a dangerous client.

   b. to involuntarily commit a dangerous client.

   c. to breach client confidentiality under exceptional circumstances.

   d. to warn anyone who is in the vicinity of the intended victim who might also be in danger.

C-169 9. _____ in a Supreme Court decision ruled that communications between licensed psychotherapists and their clients are privileged and therefore protected from forced disclosure in cases arising under federal law.

    a. Bradley Center v. Wessner

    b. Jablonski v. United States

  *c. Jaffee v. Redmond

    d. Hedlund v. Superior Court

A-170 10. Jolene tells her counselor that she is depressed about the break-up of her relationship and "just wishes she could go to sleep and never wake up." In this case, the counselor needs to

    a. immediately commit Jolene to a psychiatric facility.

  *b. assess if Jolene is suicidal and intervene if necessary.

    c. recognize that her statement is only a "cry for help" and should not be taken seriously.

    d. see if there is any chance for reconciliation.

C-173 11. The following would be an ineffective way of managing a client's suicidal ideation.

    a. Attempt to secure a promise from the client that he or she will not try to commit suicide.

    b. Immediately hospitalize the client.

  *c. Be willing to communicate your caring without setting limits.

    d. Recognize the limits of your competence and know when and how to refer.

C-175 12. Two processes that offer safeguards against malpractice liability in suicidal cases are

  *a. consultation and documentation

    b. assessment and orientation

    c. intervention and hospitalization

    d. diagnosis and informed consent

C-176 13. In regards to suicide, Szasz believes that mental-health professionals

    a. have an absolute professional duty to try to prevent suicide.

    b. should support suicide prevention policies.

    *c. need to abstain from empowering agents of the state from using coercive means to prevent when an individual chooses to end his or her life.

    d. need to document their client's suicide ideation.

C-179 14. According to the Tarasoff decision, the therapist does *not*

    a. need to accurately diagnose the client's tendency to behave in dangerous ways toward others before notifying authorities.

    *b. have a duty to warn the next of kin of suicidal patients.

    c. have the right to break confidentiality even if the client is a threat to self or others.

    d. need to be concerned about liability after notifying authorities of their client's threat to harm self or others.

C-179 15. Privileged communication does *not* apply in cases of

    a. clients' disclosures of personal and sensitive information.

    *b. child abuse and neglect.

    c. unfaithfulness in one or both partners in couple's therapy.

    d. legal proceedings where the therapist is asked to produce a client's records in court.

A-180 16. An African-American woman was interacting with her child in a domestic abuse shelter where she was overheard to say to her child, "Keep touching that and I'm going to whoop you." The social worker who heard this statement should

    a. immediately report the mother to Child Protective Services.

    b. tell the mother that she will be evicted from the shelter if she continues to talk to her child that way.

  *c. recognize that what constitutes abuse in one culture may not be viewed as abuse in another culture and not reportable until it is determined that the child is in danger.

    d. remove the child from the mother's care until the mother can learn how to talk to her child with respect.

A-182 17. A single father reports that he had too much to drink and harshly spanked his three-year-old son when he wouldn't stop screaming. The father feels terrible about the incident and asks his counselor to get some help for him so that it will never happen again. Acting on the highest level of ethical functioning, the counselor would

    a. place the child in foster care until the father can learn to deal more constructively with his anger.

    b. consult with a colleague about referring her client to a treatment center.

  *c. examine all the factors and special circumstances of this case before acting.

    d. immediately report the incident to Child Protection Services in order to protect the child.

C-184 18. A counselor working in an AIDS-related case

    a. has a legal duty to warn according to the Tarasoff decision.

    b. is obliged to protect all third parties of the threat of HIV transmission according to ethical codes.

    c. must report the case to the Department of Public Health.

  *d. has few legal guidelines to help them determine when or how to inform a potential victim of the threat of HIV transmission.

C-188 19.   The following is a proposed ethical guideline for deciding when to disclose confidential information about a client's HIV status.

    a.   When there is suspicion that there is risk of harm to a third party.

    *b. When the third party is at risk of death or substantial bodily harm.

    c.   Third parties must be warned even where there is a state law that prohibits warning.

    d.   After there is an attempt to educate the client about high risk behavior.

C-189 20.   In the case of disclosing confidential information when working with an HIV client, several writers state that therapist has a duty to protect when the following condition exists:

    a.   The client is engaging in safe-sex with a committed partner.

    *b. Clear and imminent danger must exist.

    c.   All potential victims must be warned, even if there have been multiple sexual partners over the years.

    d.   All persons who have exchanged needles with the client must be found and warned of possible danger.

Test Questions for Chapter 6

ISSUES IN THEORY, PRACTICE, AND RESEARCH

C-196 1.   Contemporary theories of counseling

    a.   are grounded on assumptions that are a part of Eastern culture.

    *b. emphasize the uniqueness of the individual, self-assertion, and ego strength.

    c.   focus on interdependence, and losing self in the totality of the cosmos.

    d.   emphasizes the social and cultural facts of human existence.

F- 198 2.   is based on a negotiation between the client and therapist to define the therapeutic relationship including specifying the goals of therapy and methods likely to be used to obtain these goals.

    a.   An agreement

  *b.   A contract

    c.   A covenant

    d.   A legally enforceable arrangement

C-200 3.   When a counselor works in a managed care system, client's goals need to be

    a.   long-term and all encompassing.

    b.   educational and therapeutic.

    c.   geared toward the client gaining insight into his or her problems and movement toward self-actualization.

  *d.   highly specific, limited to reduction of problematic symptoms, and often aimed at teaching coping skills.

F-201 4.   is a general term covering the process of identifying an emotional or behavioral problem and making a statement about the current status of a client.

    a.   Medical diagnosis

    b.   Differential diagnosis

  *c.   Psychodiagnosis

    d.   Individual diagnosis

C-201 5.   Practitioners who argue *against* diagnosis

  *a.   view it as an inappropriate application of the medial model of mental health to counseling and therapy.

    b.   are likely to be psychoanalytically-oriented therapists.

    c.   usually have a behavioristic orientation.

    d.   are likely to work for a managed care system.

C-204   6.   Therapists who fall into the category of clinicians who see diagnosis as being restrictive or who oppose diagnosis are likely to be

   a.   directive therapists.
   * b. existential or relationship-oriented therapists.
   c.   psychoanalytic therapists.
   d   those who practice from a multicultural framework.

C-204   7.   The following is *not* true concerning therapeutic use of the DSM-IV to diagnose clients.

   a.   Emphasis is on pathology, deficits, limitations, problems, and symptoms.
   b.   It deals largely with culture-bound syndromes.
   c.   It is based on the assumption that distress in a family or social context is the result of individual pathology.
   *d. It is based on a systemic approach that views the source of distress as being within the entire system, rather than on the individual.

A-206   8.   Mary is seeking counseling for relationship problems from her managed care facility. Her issues revolve around caretaking and the counselor is sure Mary can be helped through some assertiveness training. Since Mary does not fit into a DSM-IV category, the ethical therapist would most likely

   a.   submit a claim using a DSM-IV category that is acceptable to the insurance company.
   b.   refuse to treat Mary because there may not be reimbursement for services rendered.
   c.   call the managed care company with a diagnosis so an appropriate treatment strategy can be recommended.
   *d. use a systems theory approach, and also submit an individual DSM diagnosis along with a comprehensive report detailing the impact of systems that affect Mary.

C-209 9. It would be appropriate to use the diagnostic category of "Dependent Personality Disorder" on

    a. Asian clients who tend to let their parents make important decisions for them.

    b. a Native American client who quit his job to go back to the reservation because his parent was dying.

    c. a Mexican-American client who is highly involved with her family even though she is married.

    *d. Caucasian college students who need to check with their parents before making any decisions, no matter how minor.

C-210 10. According to professional ethical principles on testing, it would be unethical for a counselor to

    *a. perform testing and assessment services for which they have not been adequately trained.

    b. develop, administer, score, interpret, or use assessment procedures that are appropriate for the situation.

    c. test within the client's socialized behavioral or cognitive patterns.

    d. consider the validity of a given test and interpret data in the context of the cultural characteristics of the client.

Test Questions for Chapter 7
MANAGING BOUNDARIES AND MULTIPLE RELATIONSHIPS

A-225 1. Joe has a counseling practice and is also teaching psychology part-time at a university. He is well liked and trusted by students and some have asked for private counseling. Joe has decided to wait until semester break before taking them on as clients. Joe is

    a. exhibiting ethical behavior by telling his students that he will counsel them at the end of the semester.

    *b. in a dual relationship with his students which may cause ethical problems.

    c. playing favoritism by not counseling all of his students.

    d. not qualified to counsel his students because he is a part-time instructor.

C-228 2. The following is true concerning dual relationships:

a. There is a clear consensus among practitioners regarding nonsexual relationships in counseling.

b. Due to the fact that there are clinical, ethical, and legal risks, all blending of roles must be avoided.

c. Objectivity in counseling is enhanced with dual relationships.

*d. Counselors need to make every effort to avoid dual relationships with clients that could impart professional judgment or increase the risk of harm to clients.

A-228 3. Ted is a counselor educator and also acts as therapeutic agent for his students' personal development since personal awareness is considered to be an intrinsic part of developing counselor skills in the program at the university in which he teaches. Ted is

a. totally unethical in attempting to guide his students toward self-awareness.

b. involved in a situation in which he will become so subjective that he will be unable to teach his students.

*c. involved in role blending which is inevitable in the process of educating and supervising counselor trainees.

d. in a situation that automatically leads to a conflict of interest.

F-229 4. Departures from commonly accepted practices that could potentially benefit clients are referred to as

a. unethical boundaries.

*b. boundary crossings.

c. boundary violations.

d. interpersonal boundaries.

83

C-230 5. The following action would maximize the risks inherent in dual or multiple relationships:

    a. Set healthy boundaries from the outset.

    b. Secure informed consent of clients and discuss with them both the potential risks and benefits of dual relationships.

    c. Document any dual relationships in clinical case notes.

  *d. Become romantically involved with the client.

C-230 6. Linda is considering developing a multiple or dual relationship with her client and it's important for Linda to remember

    a. that all multiple relationships should be avoided because they are usually harmful.

    b. that absolute answers are available to resolve dual or multiple relationship dilemmas.

    c. to be cautious in order to protect oneself from censure.

  *d. to consider whether the potential benefit outweighs the potential for harm.

C-231 7. In regards to boundaries in the counseling relationship, Lazarus took the position that

  * a. certain ethics and boundaries actually diminish therapeutic effectiveness.

    b. all boundaries should be eliminated because they destroy the counseling relationship.

    c. strong boundaries must be maintained in order to avoid malpractice suits.

    d. traits such as flexibility, spontaneity, and warmth tend to be characteristics of therapists who maintain strong boundaries.

C-234 8. A professional entering into a bartering relationship, should do so only if

    a. the client indicates that they don't have the funds to continue therapy.

    b. it involves an exchange of services.

    c. it does not involve a dual relationship.

    *d. the relationship is not exploitative.

C-236 9. Therapists who are considering entering into a bartering arrangement would do well to consider all of the following recommendations *except:*

    a. Evaluate whether the bartering arrangement will put the therapist at risk of impaired professional judgment.

    b. Determine the value of the goods or services in a collaborative fashion with the client at the onset of the bartering arrangement.

    *c. Allow the bartering arrangement to continue throughout the therapeutic relationship.

    d. Document the bartering arrangement, including the value of goods or services and a date on which the arrangement will end.

A-238 10. Marty is counseling with an Asian client who recently returned from a trip to Japan to visit relatives. His client wants to give him an inexpensive souvenir. It is important for Marty to

    a. refuse the gift on ethical grounds.

    b. explain that the gift would change their relationship and create a conflict of interest.

    *c. be aware that accepting the gift is culturally appropriate with this client.

    d. explain that he cannot accept the gift until the counseling relationship is over.

C-240 11. The counselor is likely to adopt stricter social boundaries and will be concerned about polluting the transference relationship if he or she is

   *a. psychoanalytically oriented.
    b. a behavioral therapist.
    c. working with culturally diverse clients.
    d. already engaged in an active social life.

C-241 12. In a survey to study sexual attraction in the client-therapist relationship, it was determined that

    a. most respondents reported never having been attracted to any client.
    b. in most cases, sexual attraction was likely to lead to sexual relations.
    c. fear of malpractice suits prohibited the therapist from acting out their attraction to clients.
   * d. most reported that even if they were attracted to a client, they refrained from having sexual relations with them.

C-242 13. A common reaction of therapists who realize that they have sexual feelings toward their clients is to

    a. feel anger at their own sexuality.
    b. speak openly about the matter to the client.
    c. investigate to see if the client feels the same.
   *d. feel guilty and fearful of losing control and being criticized.

C-243 14. Therapists can deal with powerful attractions to clients by

    a. repressing their feelings of attraction.
    b. asking the client if the feeling is mutual.
    c. terminating the relationship immediately.
   *d. monitoring boundaries by setting clear limits on physical contact, self-disclosure, and client requests for personal information.

C-247 15. When the client is put in the position of becoming the emotional caretaker of the counselor's needs they have become victims of

    a.   covert abuse.

    b.   overt abuse.

  *c.   psychological abuse.

    d.   emotional abuse.

A-249 16. Bonnie became sexually involved with her therapist soon after therapy began. This action was initiated by the therapist who saw Bonnie's provocative behavior as an invitation to become intimate. The following is a possible on-going consequence for the client being sexually exploited:

    a.   substance abuse

    b.   suicidal ideation

    c.   distrust for therapists and the therapeutic process

    d.   impaired social adjustment and distrust of opposite sex

  *e.   all of the above

C-251 17. Clients can file a legal complaint against a therapist for sexual misconduct by

    a.   filing an ethical complaint with the therapist's professional association.

    b.   filing an ethical complaint with the therapist's licensing board.

    c.   lodging a complaint with the therapist's employer.

  *d.   filing a criminal complaint or a civil suit.

C-253 18. According to professional codes of ethics, sexual relationships between client and counselor are considered to be ethical if

    a.   the therapist is really in love with their client.

    b.   there is consent by the client.

  *c.   they are not considered to be ethical under any circumstances.

    d.   the therapeutic relationship has ended and a referral has been given.

A-254 19. Robert is romantically attracted to his client and he suspects that the feeling is mutual. In order to take an ethical action, Robert should

*a. seek consultation with an experienced colleague, supervisor, or personal therapist who could help decide a course of action.

b. terminate therapy so they can develop a romantic relationship.

c. repress his feelings and continue therapy with the client.

d. explore his reasons for the attraction and tell the client why he was attracted to her.

C-256 20. In the author's view, non-erotic touching between counselor and client should be

*a. a spontaneous and honest expression of the therapist's feelings.

b. incongruent with what they feel.

c. a therapeutic technique used to extinguish catharsis.

d. considered unethical.

Test Questions for Chapter 8

PROFESSIONAL COMPETENCE AND TRAINING

C-266 1. The following statement would *not* be true in regards to professional codes of ethics in regards to counselor competence.

a. Practitioners are required to practice within the boundaries of their competence.

* b. Only when therapists complete a doctoral program are they competent to practice with all specialties.

c. The practitioner can develop competency by working with professionals with more experience.

d. Conferences, workshops, and continuing education are means toward developing competency.

C-270 2. According to the authors, a good training program encourages students to

    *a. build on their life experiences and personal strengths and provides opportunities of expanding self-awareness.

    b. emphasize skill training without consideration of personal development.

    c. achieve a high enough GPA to pursue a doctorate.

    d. specialize in one theory with the techniques and strategies that are unique to that theory.

A-271 3. James has applied to a counselor training program at a university. He is being oriented to the program according to ACA's guidelines which state that he would *not* need to be informed of the following.

    a. The type and level of skill acquisition required for successful completion of the training.

    b. The type of student and supervisee evaluation and dismissal policies and procedures.

    c. Training components that encourage self-growth or self-disclosure as part of the training process.

    *d. The diversity of students applying to the program.

C-272 4. The argument for teaching a multimodal, systematic, technically eclectic model in training programs is that

    *a. the variety of techniques and strategies taught can be applied to a wide range of problems with diverse clients.

    b. it gives the student an opportunity to specialize in one theoretical approach.

    c. there are few bureaucratic constraints when teaching this type of approach.

    d. the student can learn to diagnose clients to fit the basic concepts of the theory being taught.

F-278 5.   _____ represents the least degree of regulation of professional practice.

    a. Certification

    b. Licensure

   *c. Registration

    d. Accreditation

C-278 6.   An argument put forth in favor of legislation to regulate the delivery of mental-health services is that

    a. professionalism builds up a rigid bureaucracy designed to protect the client.

   *b. the public is protected by setting minimum standards of service and holding professionals accountable.

    c. there are as many certified charlatans as there are uncertified, competent practitioners.

    d. it contributes to professional specializations that pit one against the other.

C-279 7.   Within the counseling profession, a specialty is officially recognized when

   *a. practitioners achieve either a specialty accreditation through a group or certification through a professional organization.

    b. the practitioner receives a doctorate degree.

    c. the counselor works in a specific area for at least two years.

    d. there is state regulation of the practice of that particular counseling specialization.

C-280 8.   In addition to the eight specialties recognized by the ACA, there is a proposal to create a new specialty in

    a. mid-life crisis counseling.

   *b. sports counseling.

    c. developmental disabilities behavioral management.

    d. incest counseling.

C-282 9. Most professional organizations support efforts to

    a. require pro bono work at the rate of at least 20% of the work week for all professionals.

    b. write regulations that encourage competition.

   *c. make continuing education a mandatory condition of relicensing.

    d. require personality tests from all practitioners to ensure that those who enter the field are in good mental health.

F-284 10. _____ is an organized system by which practitioners within a profession assess one another's services.

    a. Networking

    b. Mentoring

    c. Monitoring

   *d. Peer review

Test Questions for Chapter 9

ISSUES IN SUPERVISION AND CONSULTATIONS

C-290 1. In order to distinguish between the ethical and legal aspects of clinical supervision, the legal aspects involve

    a. supervisors' qualifications, along with their duties and responsibilities.

    b. issues with dual relationships.

    c. consent of trainees, clients, and third-party payers.

   *d. issues related to confidentiality, liability, the supervisor's duty to protect, and standards of care.

C-291   2.   Supervisees in training programs do *not* have the right to

    a.   be fully informed of their supervisor's approaches to supervision.

    b.   continual access to any records maintained during the supervisory relationship.

    *c.   expect that the supervisor will be their personal therapist if needed.

    d.   confidentiality with regard to disclosure, unless mandated by law.

C-292   3.   Supervisors are ethically vulnerable because

    a.   there is a power differential between the participants.

    b.   of the "therapy like" quality of the supervisory relationship.

    c.   they are faced with protecting the welfare of clients, supervisees, the public and the profession.

    *d.   all of the above.

C-292   4.   It is *not* the responsibility of the supervisor to

    a.   perform the role of teacher, counselor, or consultant as they are appropriate.

    b.   promote knowledge and skills required to effectively work with clients from culturally diverse backgrounds.

    c.   assist supervisees to recognize their personal limitations and protect the welfare of their clients.

    *d.   independently decide the needs of the trainee, including the course of therapy they will need.

A-294   5.   Amy is in a counselor training program and has clients that she sees on a regular basis. Since she is a counselor trainee under supervision, Amy does *not* have to

    a.   get informed consent from her client.

    b.   inform the client that she is a trainee.

    c.   be confidential with client information.

    *d.   share client information with her supervisor.

C-295 6. Although the following is an important aspect of counseling it is *not* imperative that the trainee's supervisor

    a. have specialized training in methods of supervision.

    b. have an in-depth knowledge of the specialty area in which they will provide supervision.

    *c. have professional certification in multicultural counseling theory and techniques.

    d. provide timely and adequate supervision while monitoring and evaluating the supervisee's competence.

A-298 7. Susan is in a counselor training program and is infatuated with her supervisor. She has indicated that she is interested in pursuing an intimate relationship. In order to provide adequate supervision for Susan, her supervisor would need to

    *a. clearly define and maintain ethical, professional, and social relationship boundaries with the student.

    b. attempt to resolve the situation therapeutically.

    c. suggest that she transfer to another training program.

    d. let Susan know that there is no possibility for intimacy until she graduates from the program.

C-301 8. Professional codes of ethics for supervisors agree that

    a. social interaction with supervisees is essential to effective counselor training.

    b. all dual or multiple relationships with supervisees are unethical.

    c. sexual relationships between supervisors and students are unethical unless the student freely consents.

    *d. supervisors occupy a position of power and should not engage in sexual relationships with the student.

93

A-305 9. Martha is in a counselor training program and often discusses personal concerns with her supervisor. The purpose of this discussion is

    a. for the supervisor to initiate a therapeutic relationship with the trainee.

   *b. to facilitate the trainee's ability to work successfully with clients.

    c. to resolve the trainee's problems so he or she works more effectively with clients.

    d. to always make a referral to personal therapy.

A-306 10. Kenneth is involved in a specialized professional process which involves sharing expertise with others in the helping professions so they can better serve their own clients. He is functioning in the role of a

    a. therapist.

   *b. consultant.

    c. supervisor.

    d. broker.

C-306 11. The following is true concerning the process of consultation:

   *a. Consultation is a temporary process aimed at helping consultees move toward autonomy and independence.

    b. Consultation is primarily aimed at dealing with personal problems rather than work concerns.

    c. There are formal ethical guidelines specific to the practice of consultation.

    d. Consultees are obliged to follow the recommendations of the consultant.

C-307 12. A major professional issue for consultants is the degree to which their personal values will have an impact on their actions and decisions in the consultation process. It is critical that

    a. difficult decisions be made for the consultees and support them with the follow-up action.

    b. the consultant investigate the goals of the organization to determine if they need to be changed.

    *c. consultants present qualifications to show that they are competent to deliver the services being contracted.

    d. consultants make consultees aware that they may be providing services that are beyond their competency.

C-316 13. A good consultant contract

    a. is general in nature until it can be determined what the problem is.

    b. leaves an open time frame until both parties are satisfied that the task has been accomplished.

    * c. is a form of legal protection for both parties and can assist in developing clear understanding of the consultation process.

    d. allows the consultant to act in combination with the role of a counselor.

Test Questions for Chapter 10

MULTICULTURAL PERSPECTIVES AND DIVERSITY ISSUES

C-319 1. The term *minority group* has come to refer to

    a. a sense of identity that stems from common ancestry, history, nationality, religion and race.

    b. any relationship between two or more diverse groups.

    *c. any category of people who have been discriminated against or subjected to unequal treatment and oppression by society largely because of their group membership.

    d. any pattern of behavior that denies access to opportunities or privileges to members of one racial group.

F-319 2. _____ counseling is any counseling relationship in which the counselor and the client belong to different cultural groups, hold different assumptions about social reality, and subscribe to different world views.

a. Culturally encapsulated

b. Ethnic-sensitive

*c. Multicultural

d. Transcultural

C-320 3. The culturally encapsulated counselor is characterized by

a. defining reality according to the client's reality.

b. showing sensitivity to cultural variations among individuals.

c. evaluating other viewpoints and making attempts to accommodate the behavior of others.

*d. defining reality according to one set of cultural assumptions.

A-323 4. A Chinese-American engineering student with traditional Asian values went to a college counselor because he was frustrated with his studies. He told the counselor that he disliked the engineering field even though his parents were proud of his career choice. The counselor encouraged him to change the course of his career without consulting his parents. The counselor is asking the student to ignore the following Asian value:

a. self-determination

b. passivity

*c. filial piety, or respect toward parents

d. academic achievement

F-329 5. Below are values associated with Eastern culture:

a. independence and assertiveness

*b. authoritarian orientation and interdependence

c. nonconformity and democratic orientation

d. innovation and freedom

C-329   6.   Statements such as "Minority groups need to take responsibility for their own predicament" and "In order to succeed, people need to stop complaining and start working." do not take environmental factors into account. These are examples of

   *a.   stereotypical beliefs.

   b.   guiding principles for action.

   c.   cultural tolerance.

   d.   challenging culture-bound values.

A-333   7.   Frank is a Native American college student who is seeking information about his career choice from a male counselor. The counselor notices that he uses very little eye contact and needs to recognize that Frank

   a.   lacks trust about the information he is receiving.

   b.   is unlikely to follow through with his suggestions.

   *c.   is likely to view direct eye contact as a lack of respect.

   d.   would be more likely to have direct eye contact if the counselor were a female.

C-335   8.   It is the authors' position that counselors would *not* work well with diverse populations if they

   a.   are open to being challenged and tested.

   b.   are flexible in applying theories to specific situations.

   *c.   believe that they are free from any racist attitudes, beliefs, and or feelings.

   d.   are comfortable with differences that exist between themselves and their clients.

A-336 9. Denise is a Euro-American social worker who is a former welfare client. She had four children when she was divorced and succeeded in completing her degree and getting off the system in four years. She is now working in a work-to-welfare program and sets similar goals for her multicultural clients. Denise's attitude and actions indicate that she

   a. believes in her client's ability to achieve and they will live up to her expectations.

   b. is well intentioned and willing to challenge her clients.

   c. can serve as a model of what her clients can accomplish with their lives—if she could do it, so could her clients.

   *d. is operating out of the majority value system and presuming that her clients want the same goals.

C-342 10. According to the authors, the first step in the process of acquiring multicultural counseling skills in a training program should be that students

   *a. take a self-exploratory class to help identify their cultural and ethnic blind spots.

   b. open themselves to people in other cultures through reading and travel.

   c. free themselves from all racist thoughts, actions, and feelings.

   d. have their value system conform with an "acceptable norm."

Test Questions for Chapter 11

THE COUNSELOR IN THE COMMUNITY

F-351 1. _____ are attempts to change the social environment to meet the needs of the population as a whole and are carried out by influencing social policy.

   a. Direct community services

   *b. Indirect community services

   c. Community organization services

   d. Community counseling services

F-351   2.   Direct client services focuses on

    *a.   outreach activities.

    b.   client advocacy.

    c.   consultation.

    d.   influencing policymakers.

C-352   3.   Counselors who work in the community need to recognize that it would be an error to

    a.   use community resources as a way to enrich therapy.

    *b.   believe that one person or group has a monopoly on the helping process.

    c.   work with client problems in their cultural context.

    d.   attend to the network of the client's support systems.

A-353   4.   Nakita is an African-American mother with four children and has been having trouble finding housing in a safe community. Lisa is her social worker and suspects that there may be racial discrimination involved and takes her to sites that she has previously screened for availability. In this case, Lisa is acting as an

    a.   evaluator.

    b.   adviser.

    *c.   advocate.

    d.   ombudsman.

C-353   5.   In this role, counselors assist clients in recognizing oppressive forces in the community as a source of their problem and teach their clients strategies for developing political power to bring about change in the clients' social and physical environment.

    *a.   change agent

    b.   consultant

    c.   adviser

    d.   advocate

C-353 6. Counselors can encourage ethnic minority clients to learn skills they can use to interact successfully with various forces in their community by acting as their

a. advocate.

b. broker.

c. advisor.

*d. consultant.

A-355 7. Tony is a recently relocated Mexican-American who is seeking help from a Spanish-speaking organization designed to meet the needs of newly arriving legal immigrants. Tony is quite depressed, but reluctant to talk to his counselor about his problems. The counselor refers him to an indigenous resource who is more likely to be trusted by Tony. He was referred to

a. a paraprofessional worker.

*b. either a folk or spiritual healer from the community.

c. an intern from a counseling program.

d. a community organizer.

A-355 8. Chong is a legal immigrant and is having post-traumatic stress symptoms as a result of his experiences in Laos. He may be reluctant to use the available counseling recourses because he

a. harbors the attitude that he should be able to take charge of his own life.

b. may perceive the resources as culturally insensitive.

c. believes that it is only for people who have extreme symptoms

*d. all of the above

C-358 9. Lay volunteers from the community receive thirty hours of training before working in the abuse shelter. They receive supervision at the site and are considered to be

a. indigenous workers.

*b. paraprofessional helpers.

c. counseling professionals.

d. professional community service workers.

C-359 10. Many professionals struggle with the issue of how to work within a system while retaining their dignity, vitality, and convictions. The most important component in any effort to bring about change is to

    *a. make an honest self-examination to determine the degree in which the "system" is actually hindering them.

    b. start the process of changing the system by speaking to the director of the organization.

    c. conduct research as to the reasons for the problems in the organization.

    d. evaluate the options in responding to unacceptable circumstances.

Test Questions for Chapter 12

ETHICAL ISSUES IN MARITAL AND FAMILY THERAPY

C-370 1. The family systems perspective is grounded on the assumption that a client's problematic behavior may be

    a. an individual problem that needs to be resolved before the family can meet in a group.

    b. the issue that is keeping the family in crisis.

    *c. a symptom of dysfunctional patterns handed down across generations.

    d. a result of the individual's maladjustment and psychosocial development.

C-371 2. According to marriage and family ethical standards, the therapist needs to

    a. focus the therapy on the identified patient.

    b. assure total confidentiality to family members who seek individual therapy sessions from the therapist.

    c. refrain from advertising their services.

    *d. maintain high standards of professional competence and integrity.

C-374 3. In a research project in which family therapists responded to a variety of ethical dilemmas, the first issue of importance when working with families was reported to be

    a. professional development activities.

    b. payment for services.

    c. sharing research results.

    *d. treating the entire family.

C-376 4. Below is an action that does *not* deviate from ethical standards of family therapy practice.

    a. treating homosexuality as pathological

    b. failing to warn potential victims of lethal threats

    c. tailoring diagnoses to meet insurance criteria

    *d. having values different from those of the family

C-377 5. According to the authors, the first order of importance of training family therapists is to

    *a. acquire self-knowledge, especially with regard to family-of-origin issues.

    b. learn basic counseling techniques to use with families and couples.

    c. learn and practice specialties such as systems theory.

    d. understand effective intervention techniques used when working with families and couples.

C-378 6. Gender sensitive models of training family therapists is aimed at

    a. raising consciousness concerning the role of cultural and ethnic factors in influencing the outlooks and behaviors of individuals and families.

    *b. overcoming trainee gender bias and sex-role stereo-typing.

    c. understanding the collaborative nature of family therapy.

    d. direct clinical contact with all members of the family system.

C-379 7. Most family therapy training programs employ both didactic and experiential methods and supervised practice. Experiential methods include

    a. classroom lectures, reading, and demonstrations.

    *b. both personal therapy and working with one's own family of origin.

    c. films and videotapes of family therapy sessions.

    d. role playing and discussion.

A-382 8. Natalie is a marital therapist who believes that marriage is a sacred institution and is dedicated to preserving marital relationships whenever possible. She is working with a couple who are attempting to resolve their problems even though they have also considered the possibility of divorce. One could expect that she

    a. would set her values aside and work with any decision that her clients chose to make about their marriage.

    b. would place the primary focus on helping each person examine what is the best course of action for themselves.

    *c. might let it be known that she believes in the preservation of marriage and would urge the couple to work on their issues.

    d. would consider divorce as a viable option if the couple is unhappy with their relationship.

C-384 9. Feminist family therapists are concerned about shifting the power balance between women and men in the family. Therefore, it is *not* likely that they would

    *a. focus exclusively on the couple's relationship.

    b. question gender-specific roles.

    c. place the same demands for change on both women and men.

    d. value the expression of emotion and nurturance in both men and women.

C-386 10. Below is a sex-biased therapist response to problems presented in couples therapy:

    a. Assuming that remaining married may not be the best choice for a women.

    b. Demonstrating equal interest in both the woman's career and the man's career.

  *c. Encouraging couples to accept the fact that child rearing is primarily the responsibility of the mother.

    d. Shows some value bias whether or not the wife or husband had an affair.

C-390 11. The authors take the following position in regards to confidentiality in marital and family therapy:

    a. "Hidden agendas" are seen as material that should be brought out into the open during a family session.

    b. Therapists should not divulge in a family session any information given to them in an individual session.

  *c. Therapists need to inform clients that any information given during private sessions will be divulged in accordance with the greatest benefit to the family.

    d. Family therapists are exempt from reporting information that could harm the family system.

Test Questions for Chapter 13

ETHICAL ISSUES IN GROUP WORK

C-398 1. The primary reason that therapy groups fit well into the managed care scene is because they

  *a. can be designed to be brief and cost-effective treatments.

    b. provide a sense of community to serve as an antidote to an impersonal culture in which many clients live.

    c. serve the purpose of teaching interpersonal skills.

    d. provide a natural laboratory that demonstrates to people that they are not alone and there is hope for creating a different life.

C-399 2. Below is an example of a group leader's basic skill competency.

    a. Identifying one's strengths, weaknesses, and values.

    b. Being able to describe the characteristics associated with the typical stages in a group's development.

  *c. Being able to open and close group sessions.

    d. Being able to describe the various roles and behaviors of group members.

F-400 3. _____ training should consist of courses in the area of abnormal psychology, psychopathology, and diagnostic assessment to assure capabilities in working with more disturbed populations.

    a. Task/work groups

    b. Guidance/psychoeducational groups

  *c. Psychotherapy groups

    d. Counseling/interpersonal-problem solving groups

C-401 4. The authors recommend at least three experiences as adjunct to a training program for group workers that would *not* include

    a. personal (private) psychotherapy.

    b. experience in group therapy, group counseling, or a personal-growth group.

  *c. recognition that professional codes, legislative mandates, and institutional policies alone will ensure competent group leadership.

    d. participation in a supervision and training group.

C-403 5. Experiential groups are considered to be an essential component of training group leaders and it is recommended that these groups

    a. function as therapy groups.

    b. are restricted to role-playing exercises.

    c. they should be voluntary and alternatives provided for those who do not wish to take part in these groups.

  *d. are led by advanced students or practitioners from outside the department rather than the course instructor.

C-404 6. _____ are good candidates for heterogeneous outpatient intensive therapy groups.

    a. Persons who are addicted to drugs or alcohol

    b. Hypochondriacs

   *c. Individuals who have interpersonal problems

    d. People with antisocial personalities

A-409 7. Gail feels like she has not accomplished what she wanted in her therapy group and has decided to leave. Gail's therapist needs to

   *a. encourage her to explain why she wants to leave to other group members.

    b. encourage her to leave before her negative attitude affects other members of the group.

    c. put undue pressure on her to stay in group.

    d. encourage other members to pressure her to stay.

C-410 8. The following is true in regards to group ethics.

   * a. As a rule, group leaders should conduct only those types of groups for which they have been trained.

    b. The legal concept of privileged communication applies in group settings the same as it applies to individual sessions.

    c. Group leaders are not obliged to inform psychiatric hospital patients that they are documenting group sessions.

    d. Parents and guardians have the legal right to all communications that have occurred in groups for minors.

C-414 9. Below is an example of a technique being used in an unethical way.

    a. Modifying techniques so they are suitable for the client's cultural and ethnic background.

   *b. Practicing unfamiliar techniques in group.

    c. Have a therapeutic purpose and be grounded in some theoretical framework.

    d. Members are given the freedom on whether or not they wish to participate in a given experiment.

A-416 10. Andy is in a grief group and seems "stuck" in his sorrow over the death of his father. The leader realizes that Andy needs to work on this issue even though the group is coming to a close. He believes that Andy could best benefit by a technique that will allow him to openly express his emotions. In this case, the group leader should make an ethical decision to

a. introduce the technique even though there is no chance to procεεs after group.

*b. recognize the potential adverse effects of techniques used to elicit emotions and take precautions to ensure that there is time to process.

c. persuade Andy to participate in the technique even if he seems reluctant, since it is essential to express grief openly.

d. make sure Andy has a good support system so he won't feel abandoned when group terminates.

PRACTICE EXAMINATION for
Issues and Ethics in the Helping Professions, Fifth Edition

Directions: These true-false examination questions are based upon the textbook, *Issues and Ethics in the Helping Professions, Fifth Edition* [1998] (Corey, Corey, and Callanan). The intent of this practice examination is to serve as a *comprehension check for your level of mastery* of the reading. By taking this test, and using it as a tool for review, you will likely improve your performance on the final examination for the course. In taking the exam, decide if the statement is "more true" or "more false." Some of the items are subject to interpretation, and the answers could vary depending on one's perspective. In the case of this type of statement or question, use the authors' perspective given in the textbook. (At times, the question includes the qualifier "According to the authors. . .")

1. Law and ethics are basically synonymous concepts.

2. Community standards (or mores) are universal, in that they apply to all mental-health disciplines, to all theories, and to all geographical areas.

3. Principle ethics typically focuses on acts and choices.

4. According to the authors, most violations of ethics probably happen quite inadvertently in counseling practice.

5. Because most ethical violations are readily detected, ethical codes are easy to enforce.

6. Ethical codes are partially designed to protect practitioners against charges of malpractice, for counselors who conscientiously practice in accordance with these codes have some measure of defense in case of legal action.

7.   The ethical codes of the professional organizations provide ready-made answers to ethical dilemmas that practitioners face.

8.   Virtue ethics asks "Am I doing what is best for my client?"

9.   The principle of nonmaleficence refers to applying the maximum professional skill and competence for promoting the growth and development of clients.

10. The principle of autonomy refers to therapists' making efforts at fostering maximum self-development on the part of clients.

11. The principle of fidelity refers to providing equal treatment to all people regardless of age, sex, race, ethnicity, disability, socio-economic status, cultural background, religion, or sexual orientation.

12.   The prinicple of veracity means that practitioners are truthful with their clients.

13.   The feminist model of ethical decision making calls for client involvement in the process of making such decisions.

14.   Therapists often report that burnout resulted from the nonreciprocated giving and the responsibility demanded by the therapeutic relationship.

15.   Transference is sometimes referred to as the "unreal" relationship in therapy.

16.   It is both possible and desirable for counselors to be scrupulously neutral with respect to values in the counseling relationship.

17.   Counselors often give clients clues about their values through their nonverbal and body messages.

18.   The authors contend that counselors who impose their values (in indirect ways) on their clients are behaving unethically.

19.   According to the authors, counselors would do well to state their own values in cases involving value conflicts between therapist and client.

110

20. Ethically, counselors should refer a client if they have not struggled with exactly the same value issue.

21. In any case where counselors do not agree with the value systems of their clients, ethical practice dictates that they refer these clients to another professional.

22. According to the authors, there is no place in counseling for discussing religious or spiritual values, as this type of discussion is best done with a minister, priest, or rabbi.

23. The authors believe that clients' values should be respected, but challenged by the therapist.

24. The authors contend that values should be kept out of therapy.

25. Informed consent is especially important when working under a managed care system.

26. Giving clients access to their files seems to be consistent with the consumer-rights movement.

27. The practice of involuntary commitment of people to mental institutions raises difficult professional, ethical, and legal issues.

28. In order for clients to develop trust in their therapist, it is essential that they know that confidentiality will not be compromised under any conditions.

29. Legally, there are three elements to adequate informed consent: autonomy, good will, and empathy.

30. The process of educating clients about their rights might well begin with having them sign informed-consent documents.

31. Confidentiality should be considered as an absolute.

32. At the outset, clients have a right to know about the benefits and the risks involved in psychological treatment.

33. One of the major obstacles to the open sharing of files with clients is the need to give clients a diagnostic classification as a requirement for receiving third-party reimbursements.

34. The ethical responsibility of counselors to safeguard clients from unauthorized disclosures of information given in the therapy relationship is the definition of privileged communication.

35. In privileged communication, the waiver belongs to the therapist.

36. When it is necessary to break confidentiality, it is not a good policy to invite the client to participate in this process.

37. Clients in a managed care program should be informed that confidentiality may be compromised under this system.

38. Generally speaking, the legal concept of privileged communication does not apply to group counseling.

39. Most of the ethical codes contain guidelines for safeguarding a client's right to privacy.

40. Therapists have both an ethical and a legal responsibility to clarify the limitations of confidentiality.

41. It is generally agreed that therapists do not have a duty to protect suicidal clients, if these clients decide that they want to take their own life.

42. The Jaffee case resulted in an extension of privileged communication for licensed psychotherapists.

43. The Hedlund case held that the therapist must accurately diagnose the client's condition for behaving in dangerous ways toward others.

44. The Jablonski case ruled that the protective privilege ends where the public peril begins.

45. It is expected that the decision in the Jaffee case will have far-reaching consequences for licensed psychotherapists and their clients.

46.   Civil liability means that an individual can be sued for not doing right or for doing wrong to another.

47.   Perhaps the best way to protect yourself from a malpractice suit is to restrict your practice to clients for whom you are prepared by virtue of your education, training, and experience.

48.   Malpractice is more of an ethical concept than a legal concept.

49.   To prevent their being sued, practitioners are expected to possess and exercise the knowledge, skill, and judgment common to other members of their profession.

50.   Violations of confidentiality and sexual misconduct have received the greatest attention in the literature as grounds for malpractice suits.

51.   In the counseling relationship dual/multiple relationships are always unethical.

52.   According to the authors, counselors who establish any form of social relationships with *former* clients are necessarily engaging in unethical practice.

53.   Counselors who become aware of sexual attractions to their clients can be sure that they are involved in countertransference.

54.   Touching that does not lead to intercourse is associated with older and more experienced therapists.

55.   The practice of bartering therapy for either goods or services is generally considered to be both unethical and illegal.

56.   In those cases when there is the potential for negative consequences arising from a dual relationship, it is the practitioner's responsibility to consult with other professionals or seek supervision.

57.   Therapist sexual involvement with clients is both unethical and illegal.

58. Concerning sexual intimacy between therapist and client, most professional organizations do not have a specific code condemning this practice.

59. Increasingly, clients are successfully suing therapists who engaged in sex with them.

60. Most codes of ethics specify that sexual intimacy with a *former* client is considered unethical before two years after termination.

61. Specialization training applies to all levels of education, from associate of arts to doctoral programs.

62. Most licenses specify the types of clients or problems the licensee is competent to work with, as well as specifying the techniques a practitioner is competent to use.

63. A major problem of the peer-review process is the difficulty in determining the qualifications of the reviewers.

64. Licensure is the most inclusive, legislatively established basis of credentiality.

65. The process of certification and licensure can be the basis for professional jealousy over turf and can lead to restrictive regulation that is motivated by competition for access to the marketplace.

66. It is considered appropriate for supervisors to provide therapy for their supervisees when they have personal problems that affect their clients.

67. Counselors are often expected to function in the roles of both supervisor and consultant.

68. Supervisors are ultimately responsible, both ethically and legally, for the actions of their trainees.

69. Trainees do not have a legal or an ethical right to periodic feedback and evaluation from their supervisor.

70. Supervisors have a legal and ethical obligation to respect the confidentiality of client communications.

71. Sexual intimacies between a supervisor and a supervisee should not be considered unethical if both parties consent.

72. The topic of competence in supervision is incomplete without taking into consideration the role of cultural factors in the supervisory relationship and the competence of supervisors in this area.

73. Supervisors themselves need supervision if they hope to enhance their own multicultural development.

74. Before initiating a contract, consultants should investigate the goals of the organization to determine whether they can support them.

75. Dual/multiple relationships do not apply in cases of consulting.

76. In using tests with minority clients, it is important to proceed with caution if the instrument was not standardized by including minority populations.

77. In order to create a meaningful research design to evaluate the outcomes of psychotherapy, it is not necessary to obtain informed consent of the clients.

78. Practitioners with a psychoanalytic orientation tend not to favor psychodiagnosis.

79. Some writers have noted that cultural factors are often neglected in both research and theory.

80. Issues in theory, practice, and research are necessarily separate and distinct.

81. Most of the ethical codes mention the practitioner's responsibility for recognizing the special needs of diverse client populations.

82. Failure to address cultural factors in counseling relationships often constitutes unethical practice.

83. Multiculturalism has been referred to as the "third force" in counseling.

84. Regardless of one's cultural background, silence in a counseling session can always be seen as a form of resistance.

85. There is a great deal of scientific evidence that supports the position that minority clients should always be treated by minority therapists.

86. Cultural tunnel vision, or cultural encapsulation, can result in unethical behavior in multicultural counseling situations.

87. It is a good policy to provide children with treatment alternatives and enlist their participation in defining goals for their therapy.

88. Most states now require specialized training in gender-sensitive therapy as a condition for relicensure.

89. In most states specialized training in counseling gay and lesbian clients is required for relicensure.

90. Virtually all states have mandatory reporting laws in cases of child abuse or suspected child abuse.

91. In child custody cases, confidentiality is limited when therapists are called on to give expert testimony.

92. At this time, there are no ethical guidelines specific to the practice of marital and family therapy.

93. From a legal perspective, members in a group generally waive privileged communication, since a third party is present.

94. There are virtually no psychological risks involved in participating in a group.

95. People have a right to know what they are getting into before they make a commitment to become a part of any group.

96. Group leaders who have not participated in their own individual and group therapy are guilty of unethical practice.

97. The community counselor focuses primarily on the person-in-the-environment.

98. Counselors working from a community perspective examine dysfunctional behavior by focusing on the dynamnics within the client that have led to the client's personal problems.

99. Outreach strategies are particularly important in reaching ethnic minorities.

100. For many ethnically diverse clients, seeking help in the form of traditional counseling is foreign.

Answer Key

1.	F	26.	T	51.	F	76.	T
2.	F	27.	T	52.	F	77.	T
3.	T	28.	F	53.	F	78.	F
4.	T	29.	F	54.	T	79.	T
5.	F	30.	T	55.	F	80.	F
6.	T	31.	F	56.	T	81.	T
7.	F	32.	T	57.	T	82.	T
8.	T	33.	T	58.	F	83.	F
9.	F	34.	F	59.	T	84.	F
10.	T	35.	F	60.	T	85.	F
11.	F	36.	F	61.	T	86.	T
12.	T	37.	T	62.	F	87.	T
13.	T	38.	T	63.	T	88.	F
14.	T	39.	T	64.	T	89.	F
15.	T	40.	T	65.	T	90.	T
16.	F	41.	F	66.	F	91.	T
17.	T	42.	T	67.	T	92.	F
18.	T	43.	F	68.	T	93.	T
19.	T	44.	F	69.	F	94.	F
20.	F	45.	T	70.	T	95.	T
21.	F	46.	T	71.	F	96.	F
22.	F	47.	T	72.	T	97.	T
23.	T	48.	F	73.	T	98.	F
24.	F	49.	T	74.	T	99.	T
25.	T	50.	T	75.	F	100.	T

FINAL EXAMINATION for
Issues and Ethics in the Helping Professions, Fifth Edition

Directions: Please use SCAN TRON [Form 884] and number 2 pencil. Leave no blanks on your answer sheet and make only one response per item. Select the one best answer. BE SURE TO RECORD THIS TEST NUMBER ON YOUR SCAN TRON SHEET AND RETURN THIS TEST WITH YOUR ANSWER SHEET TO THE INSTRUCTOR DIRECTLY.

MULTIPLE CHOICE QUESTIONS

Below are 150 multiple choice items. Decide on the ONE BEST response. Leave no blanks and erase clearly and make no stray marks. **Note:** Some of the test items might be subject to interpretation. In these cases, consider the perspective given by the authors of the textbook.

CHAPTER 1—Introduction to Professional Ethics

1. Ethical issues in the mental-health professions are regulated
   a. by legislation.
   *b. by professional codes.
   c. both by legislation and professional codes.

2. Law and ethics
   a. are two distinct entities.
   *b. share common elements.
   c. are synonymous.

3. The first level of ethical functioning is characterized by compliance with the law and by following the ethical codes. This is called
   a. personal ethics.
   b. ideal ethics.
   c. aspirational ethics.
   *d. mandatory ethics.
   c. basic ethics.

4. A higher level of ethical functioning is sometimes known as
   a. personal ethics.
   b. ideal ethics.
   *c. aspirational ethics.
   d. mandatory ethics.
   e. basic ethics.

5. What is *not* a limitation of professional codes of ethics?
   a. There are conflicts within codes and between them.
   b. Codes are the basis of most institutional policies and practices.
   *c. Some issues cannot be handled by ethical codes alone.
   d. Ethics defines the minimum standards society will tolerate

6. Which of the following statements is *not* correct?
   *a. Codes are intended to be a blueprint that would remove the need for the use of judgment and ethical reasoning.
   b. Ethical codes tend to be conservative by nature.
   c. Codes were developed to protect the profession from outside regulation, and thus they reflect what most professionals can agree on.
   d. Final authority must rest with the practitioners in making decisions.
   e. Ethical codes need to be understood within a cultural framework, and therefore they must be adapted to specific cultures.

7. Community standards

    *a. may serve as the legal criteria for determining whether a practitioner provided an acceptable standard of care.

    b. always dictate the development of ethical codes.

    c. are the only basis for making sound ethical decisions.

    d. are more rigorous than ethical standards.

    e. are essentially the same thing as ethical standards.

8. Principle ethics

    *a. focuses on the use of rational, objective, universal, and impartial principles in the analysis of ethical dilemmas.

    b. focuses on the character traits of the counselor.

    c. asks the question "Am doing what is best for my client?"

    d. is the highest level of ethical standards expected of a counselor.

9. Virtue ethics asks which of the following questions?

    a. Is what I am doing legal?

    b. Is this situation unethical?

    *c. Am I doing what is best for my client?

    d. Is there a basic conflict between the ethical and legal course.

    e. How can I best protect myself from a malpractice suit?

10. The following principle implies avoidance of doing harm, which includes refraining from actions that risk hurting clients:

    a. autonomy.

    b. beneficence.

    *c. nonmaleficence.

    d. justice, or fairness.

    e. veracity

11. This principle refers to therapists making efforts at fostering maximum self-determination on the part of clients:

 *a. autonomy.

  b. beneficence.

  c. nonmaleficence.

  d. justice, or fairness.

  e. fidelity

12. This principle refers to providing equal treatment to all clients, regardless of age, sex, race, ethnicity, disability, cultural background, religion, or lifestyle:

  a. autonomy.

  b. beneficence.

  c. nonmaleficence.

 *d. justice, or fairness.

  e. fidelity

13. This principle refers to applying the maximum professional skill and competence for promoting the growth and development of clients:

  a. autonomy.

 *b. beneficence.

  c. nonmaleficence.

  d. justice, or fairness.

  e. veracity

14. Of the following steps in making an ethical decision, which one step would most likely be the *initial step* taken by a practitioner in resolving an ethical dilemma?

  a. Enumerate the consequences of various decisions.

  b. Consider possible and probable courses of action.

  c. Obtain consultation.

 *d. Identify the problem, or dilemma.

  e. Review the relevant ethical guidelines.

15. Which of the following would be the *last step* when making an ethical decision?

    a. Obtain consultation.

  *b. Decide on what appears to be the best course of action.

    c. Enumerate the consequences of various decisions.

    d. Identify the potential issues involved.

    e. Check with an attorney to prevent a malpractice suit.

CHAPTER 2—The Counselor as a Person and as a Professional

16. Concerning the issue of unresolved personal conflicts, the authors take the position that

  *a. the personal needs of a therapist can interfere with the therapeutic process if the therapist is unaware of these needs.

    b. therapists must resolve all their personal difficulties before they begin to counsel others.

    c. counselors must have experienced exactly the same problems as their clients in order to have empathy for their clients.

    d. none of the above.

17. What would *not* be a good rationale for therapy for the therapist?

    a. Those who counsel others should know what the experience of being a client is like.

    b. Therapy can assist the helper in becoming aware of his needs and motivations.

    c. Therapy can clarify our values as they apply to the therapy process.

  *d. In order to be an effective therapist, he or she must be free of blind spots and resolve all his or her unfinished business.

18. Transference is sometimes referred to as the "unreal" relationship in therapy. This implies that

    a. transference is merely a figment in the client's imagination.

  *b. the client's projections are erroneous.

    c. therapy is an artificial relationship.

    d. transference is not an important issue in therapy.

19. Holzman, Searight, and Hughes (1996) conducted a survey about experience on personal therapy among clinical psychology graduate students. What did they find?

    a. Most therapist did not view personal therapy as being important for practicing as a therapist.

    b. Most of them entered therapy because it was required of their graduate program.

    c. Most of the respondents resented being required to seek personal therapy.

  *d. Nearly 75% reported receiving personal therapy at some point in their lives, but mostly during graduate school.

    e. The average length of treatment was six therapy sessions.

20. Countertransference is best considered as

    a. feelings of genuine concern of the therapist for clients.

    b. the client's projections toward the therapist.

  *c. any projections by a therapist that can potentially get in the way of helping a client.

    d. empathy demonstrated by the therapist for the client.

    e. normal feelings of therapists toward clients.

21. Countertransference becomes an ethical issue when the

  *a. client's needs assume priority over the therapist's needs.

    b. counselor's unresolved conflicts get in the way of effective therapy.

    c. client uses session time to work through his or her problems.

    d. client puts all the blame for their difficulties on the therapist.

22. Which of the following is *not* listed as a form of countertransference?
    a. development of sexual or romantic feelings
    b. being overprotective with clients
    c. the need for constant reinforcement and approval
    *d. having genuine empathy for clients
    e. compulsive advice giving

23. In studies of therapists, which of the following was reported as the most stressful source of client behavior for therapists?
    a. clients' premature termination
    *b. suicidal statements
    c. apathy or lack of motivation
    d. anger toward the therapist
    e. agitated anxiety

24. Delaying the termination of a client by a therapist can be considered
    a. an attempt to help clients work through stubborn resistances.
    *b. a form of fostering client dependence.
    c. a form of transference on the client's part.
    d. a measure of preventing malpractice suits.
    e. a legal requirement to provide a standard of care to the client.

25. Stress of mental-health professionals is primarily related to
    a. events that occur in the therapist's work.
    *b. irrational or unrealistic beliefs that many therapists hold.
    c. failure to have experienced their own therapy.
    d. the motivation of their clients to cooperate with therapy.

26. Professionals who are *not* at a high risk of burnout include
    *a. those who get most of their personal needs met through their social life outside of work.
    b. those who assume *unreasonable* responsibility for client outcomes.
    c. those who limit their work to one type of activity.
    d. those who work with very demanding clients.

125

27. The most common characteristic of the impaired practitioner is

    a. empathy.

  *b. denial.

    c. a high level of self-esteem.

    d. the willingness to offer pro bono services for clients who cannot afford therapy.

    e. a satisfactory level of intimacy in his or her own life.

28. Impaired counselors

    a. have the ability to resolve stressful events.

    b. are able to function professionally.

  *c. experience deterioration of therapeutic skills.

    d. are able to alleviate the suffering of their clients.

29. Which of the following statements is true about the impaired professional?

  *a. Many counselors have avoided or denied the existence of the impairment issue.

    b. Much is known about the impact of impairment on clients.

    c. There is extensive research on counselor impairment.

    d. There are many professionally sponsored avenues to helping impaired professionals.

30. From the authors' perspective, what should students in a counseling program be told about the profession they are about to enter?

    a. Counseling can be a hazardous profession.

    b. Because practitioners use their own life experiences in their work, they are vulnerable to reexperiencing old wounds.

    c. There are stresses both from the nature of therapeutic work and from role expectations of therapists.

    d. Working with clients can open up the therapist's own issues.

  *e. all of the above

31. To the question "Is it possible for counselors to keep their values out of their counseling sessions?" the authors take the position that

    a. it is possible for counselors to be neutral with respect to values in the counseling relationship.

    b. it is desirable for counselors to be value neutral.

    *c. it is neither possible nor desirable for counselors to be neutral with respect to values in the counseling relationship.

    d. counselors should keep their values hidden so that they won't contaminate their clients' choices.

    e. it is the counselors' job to influence their clients to adopt proper values.

32. Imposing of the counselor's values on a client is

    a. illegal.

    *b. generally considered unethical.

    c. both illegal and unethical.

    d. necessary when the client's values are in conflict with the counselor's values.

33. Counselors can influence their clients' values by

    a. paying attention and reinforcing certain aspects of what their clients disclose.

    b. their nonverbal behavior.

    c. asking leading questions.

    *d. all of the above

34. Ethically, counselors should refer a client when they

    a. have sharp value conflicts with clients.

    *b. are likely to persuade their clients to adopt a particular point of view.

    c. have not struggled with exactly the same value issue.

    d. do not experience warmth towards their clients.

35. Regarding the issue of differences in life experiences, the authors take the position that counselors need *not*

    a. have a personal connection with their clients unless they have had similar life experiences.

    b. to be sensitive to the differences in their backgrounds.

    *c. have experienced each of the struggles of their clients to be effective in working with them.

    d. be concerned with past life experiences since they are working in the here-and-now.

36. In the Jensen and Bergin (1988) national survey of value orientations of mental-health practitioners, they found a consensus of certain values as guiding the course of psychotherapy. Which one of the following was *not* one of these values?

    a. developing the ability to give and to receive affection

    b. having a sense of purpose for living

    c. finding satisfaction in one's life

    *d. striving for financial success

    e. being able to practice self-control

37. The practitioners in the above survey did *not* view the values they identified as

    a. being central to mentally healthy lifestyles.

    b. a basis for guiding and evaluating the course of therapy.

    c. being universal values.

    *d. being relative values.

38. A way to minimize significantly the ethically questionable conversion of others to your values is to

    a. inform yourself about the varieties of values held in society.

    b. be aware of your own values.

    c. present value options in an unbiased manner.

    d. respect clients who have values different from yours.

    *e. all of the above

39. Most writers in the chapter on values tend to agree on which following principle?

    a. Therapists have the ultimate task of deciding what is best for their clients.

    *b. Therapists have a role in promoting self-determination as a value for clients.

    c. If therapists have value differences with their clients, they should do what they can to convert their clients toward their own values.

    d. Under no circumstances is it appropriate for therapists to disclose their values to their clients, lest they sway them.

40. From the perspective of the authors, what is *not* role of values in therapy?

    a. Values are a crucial part of the therapy process.

    *b. Clients' values should never be challenged, by the therapist.

    c. Therapists need to consider why the client is seeking therapy.

    d. Values influence the direction of therapy.

CHAPTER 4—Client Rights and Counselor Responsibilities

41. Most of the codes of ethics state that informed consent is required

    a. only for voluntary clients.

    b. only for involuntary clients.

    c. only for adults.

    *d. as a prerequisite for most forms of assessment and treatment.

42. The ethics codes specify that informed consent

    a. is best completed at the initial meeting with a client.

    b. is accomplished before the client comes in for the initial session.

    *c. begins when counseling is initiated and continues throughout the counseling process as necessary.

    d. is done only when the client requests it.

    e. is best initiated after several counseling sessions.

43. Which of the following is *not* a necessary legal element for adequate informed consent?

   *a.   autonomy
   b.   capacity
   c.   comprehension of information
   d.   voluntariness

44. Informed consent procedures should have all but which of the following?

   a.   costs
   *b.   a precise definition of every technique that may be used in therapy
   c.   the length of therapy
   d.   background of the therapist
   e.   alternatives to traditional therapy

45. Student counselors generally meet regularly with their supervisors and fellow students to discuss their progress in any problems they encounter in their work. This practice

   a.   is unethical, but not illegal.
   b.   shows that a counselor is technically incompetent.
   *c.   is a good policy for counselors to inform their clients that this is likely to occur.
   d.   violates the client's confidentiality.

46. Giving clients access to their files

   *a.   seems to be consistent with the consumer-rights movement.
   b.   is an invitation to a malpractice suit.
   c.   is legally, professionally, and ethically inappropriate.
   d.   is generally unethical, but not generally illegal.
   e.   should be done routinely for seriously disturbed clients.

47. One of the major obstacles to the open sharing of files with clients is
    a. the fact that doing so is against the policy of agencies.
    b. the danger of being vulnerable to a lawsuit by giving a client too much information.
    *c. the reluctance of clients to give their consent for seeing their own files.
    d. the need to give clients a diagnostic classification as a requirement for receiving third-party reimbursement.

48. Educating clients about the treatment process might well include exploring
    a. what services the therapist will provide.
    b. how long the will treatment last.
    c. the behavior expected of the client.
    d. what financial considerations need to be taken into account.
    *e. all of the above

49. For a practitioner who works under a managed care system, clients have a right to know that
    a. they will have access to needed care that extends beyond their benefits.
    *b. financial incentives exist to keep the amount or type of service limited.
    c. the number of sessions that are allowed will be determined by the type of therapy needed by the client.
    d. the system will have no access to their records.

50. If tape recording or videotaping of sessions is done, ethical practice dictates that
    a. clients have a right to be informed about this procedure at the initial session.
    b. clients understand why and how these recording will be used.
    c. secret recordings will not be made.
    d. who will have access to the tapes.
    * e. all of the above

131

51.   Which of the following is an alternative to traditional therapy?
   *a.   peer self-help groups
   b.   behavior therapy
   c.   group therapy
   d.   psychodynamic therapy

52.   Proponents of using therapeutic contracts emphasize the
   *a.   collaborative partnership of client and therapist.
   b.   need for therapists to employ manipulation to uproot client defenses.
   c.   value of keeping the therapeutic process mysterious.
   d.   value of therapists promoting client dependence.
   e.   the need to keep clients passive during the therapy process.

53.   Regarding giving clients information about the possible benefits and risks of a treatment program, it is a good idea to
   a.   avoid talking about these issues too early in therapy, lest clients become needlessly anxious.
   b.   give clients promises of specific outcomes, if they cooperate with the program.
   *c.   emphasize the role of client responsibility for outcomes.
   d.   avoid talking about risks, but play up the benefits of therapy.

54.   Which of the following would least likely be a part of the content of the informed consent process?
   a.   background of the therapist
   *b.   testimonials from prior clients
   c.   the length of therapy and termination
   d.   the fact that consultation may occur with colleagues
   e.   interruptions in therapy

55. The *main* purpose for maintaining client records is for
    a. reimbursement by an insurance carrier.
    b. the protection of a therapist against a lawsuit.
    *c. the benefit of the client.
    d. conducting research on the process and outcome of therapy.
    e. meeting the requirements of managed care policies.

56. In absence of a state law, *complete* clinical records would be kept for a minimum of
    a. one year.
    *b. three years.
    c. eight years.
    d. twelve years.
    e. as long as the client is alive.

57. Therapists who work with children and adolescents must
    a. often function as advocates for their under-age clients.
    b. know the laws of their state.
    c. struggle with dealing with confidentiality issues.
    d. be willing to seek consultation in difficult ethical and legal situations.
    *e. all of the above

58. What can a therapist do to avoid malpractice suits?
    a. use some form of a diagnostic system
    b. maintain prudent and reasonable practices in working with clients
    c. make use of informed consent
    d. keep adequate clinical records, documenting key aspects of therapy
    *e. all of the above

59. One of the *best* ways to protect yourself from a malpractice suit is to

　　*a. restrict your practice to clients for whom you are prepared by virtue of your education, training, and experience.

　　b. insist that your clients sign a contract at the outset of therapy.

　　c. tape record the counseling sessions.

　　d. carry professional liability insurance.

　　e. keep detailed notes.

60. Which condition is *not* essential for malpractice litigation?

　　a. The therapist must have a duty to the client.

　　b. The therapist must act in a negligent or improper manner.

　　c. There must be a causal relationship between that negligence and the damage claimed by the client.

　　*d. The therapist must have engaged in illegal behavior.

61. Of the following which is the *major* cause of malpractice suits against mental-health professionals?

　　a. misrepresenting one's professional training and skills

　　b. the failure to keep adequate records

　　c. accepting gifts from clients

　　*d. sexual misconduct

　　e. faulty diagnosis

62. Therapists cannot protect themselves from malpractice suits when they

　　*a. don't keep records so their notes or observations cannot be used against them in court.

　　b. clearly define issues pertaining to fees at the outset of therapy.

　　c. consult with colleagues when they are in doubt.

　　d. refuse to accept gifts from your clients.

　　e. make use of informed-consent procedures.

63. What is essential to remember in consulting with others about a specific client?

    a. Tell the client of your reasons for wanting to consult.

    b. Inquire about the client's reactions to your proposed consultation.

    c. Obtain written consent from the client for the release of information.

  *d. all of the above

64. In case you are involved in a malpractice suit, what should you do?

    a. Destroy or alter any files that could incriminate you.

    b. Discuss the case with as many people as possible to get ideas of what to do next.

    c. Seek out the client who is suing you and attempt to change his or her mind.

  *d. Seek consultation with an attorney.

    e. Continue the professional relationship with the client who is suing you, lest you be charged with abandonment.

65. Which of the following is *not* a trend in legal liability?

    a. Malpractice suits will be more effective against those therapeutic approaches that are highly directive and active.

    b. Family therapy will prompt suits by family members who are dissatisfied with the outcomes.

  *c. Private practitioners are less vulnerable to litigation than they were in the past.

    d. There will be an increase in the use of informed-consent doctrine in cases of negligence.

    e. There will be an increase in suits over approaches that have not been effective as short-term therapies.

CHAPTER 5—Confidentiality: Ethical and Legal Issues

66. The legal right which exists by statute and which protects the client from having his confidences revealed publicly from the witness stand during legal proceedings without his or her permission is the definition of
    a. confidentiality.
    *b. privileged communication.
    c. privacy.
    d. informed consent

67. The ethical responsibility of mental-health professionals to safe-guard clients from unauthorized disclosures of information given in the therapeutic relationship is the definition of
    *a. confidentiality.
    b. privileged communication.
    c. privacy.
    d. informed consent

68. The freedom of individuals to choose for themselves the time, place, manner, and extent of sharing oneself with others is the definition of
    a. confidentiality.
    b. privileged communication.
    *c. privacy.
    d. informed consent

69. In privileged communication,
    a. the waiver belongs to the therapist.
    *b. the waiver belongs to the client.
    c. the waiver belongs to either the therapist or client, depending on the case involved.
    d. the therapist has the right to invoke the privilege against the client's wishes.

70. Since the therapist/client privilege is a legal concept, which of the following is a circumstance in which information must be provided by the therapist?
    a. when the therapist is acting in a court-appointed capacity
    b. when the client initiates a lawsuit against the therapist
    c. when the therapist determines that the client is in need of hospitalization
    *d. all of the above

71. When it becomes necessary to break confidentiality,
    a. it is wise to try to keep this from the client so as not to arouse suspicion and negatively affect the relationship.
    *b. it is a good practice to inform the client of the intention to take this action.
    c. it is unwise to invite the client to participate in this process.
    d. the therapist should refer the client to another professional.
    e. the therapist should reveal the maximum amount of information possible.

72. Which of the following is *not* one of the legal trends in confidentiality?
    a. There are ethical grounds for the safeguarding of confidentiality.
    *b. Confidentiality can be absolutely ensured under a legal framework.
    c. How counselors carry out this professional obligation is increasingly being specified by law.
    d. The therapeutic process seems to proceed adequately without the existence of absolute confidentiality.

73. Which of the following statements is *not* true as it relates to the issue of confidentiality?

    a.   The counselor has a responsibility to explain the degree of confidentiality they can promise.

    *b. It is seen as ethical to break confidentiality when child abuse is suspected, but it is not a legal requirement in most states.

    c.   Confidentiality cannot be considered an absolute.

    d.   Accepted ethical standards do not clearly define circumstances when confidentiality should be broken.

    e.   Confidentiality must be broken in cases where the client is a danger to themselves and others.

74. Legally, confidentiality must be broken

    a.   when an employers requests records.

    b.   when an insurance company is paying for treatment.

    c.   if records are subpoenaed into court.

    *d. when the client is a threat to self or others.

75. The responsibility to protect the public from dangerous acts of violent clients entails liability for civil damages when practitioners neglect this duty by

    a.   failing to diagnose or predict dangerous behavior.

    b.   failing to warn potential victims of violent behavior.

    c.   failing to commit dangerous individuals.

    d.   prematurely discharging dangerous clients from the hospital.

    *e. all of the above

76. Which case dealt with the duty *not* to negligently release a dangerous patient?

    a.   the Tarasoff case

    *b. the Bradley case

    c.   the Jablonski case

    d.   the Hedlund case

    e.   the Jaffee case

77. Which case dealt with the decision holding that the therapist must accurately diagnose the client's condition for behaving in dangerous ways toward others, and so not allow negligent release?

   a.   the Tarasoff case

   *b.   the Bradley case

   c.   the Jablonski case

   d.   the Hedlund case

   e.   the Jaffee case

78. The following guiding principle was the basis for the decision in which court case? "The public policy favoring protection of the confidential character of patient-psychotherapist communications must yield to the extent to which disclosure is essential to avert danger to others. The protective privilege ends where the public peril begins."

   *a.   the Tarasoff case

   b.   the Bradley case

   c.   the Jablonski case

   d.   the Hedlund case

   e.   the Jaffee case

79. The duty to warn not only the potential victim, but also anyone who might be near the intended victim, and who might also be in danger, was affirmed by the

   a.   Tarasoff case.

   b.   Bradley case.

   c.   Jablonski case.

   *d.   Hedlund case.

   e.   Jaffee case.

80. Which case underscores the duty to commit a dangerous individual and therapist's negligence for failure to commit?
   a. the Tarasoff case
   b. the Bradley case
   *c. the Jablonski case
   d. the Hedlund case
   e. the Jaffee case

81. Which case represented a victory for mental health organizations, since it extended the confidentiality privilege for licensed psychotherapists?
   a. the Tarasoff case
   b. the Bradley case
   c. the Jablonski case
   d. the Hedlund case
   *e. the Jaffee case

82. Which of the following is *not* one of the characteristics associated with suicide-prone behavior?
   *a. The suicide rate for women is about three times greater than that of men.
   b. Up to 80% of suicides were preceded by a prior attempt.
   c. Feelings of hopelessness and depression tend to be associated with suicidal intentions.
   d. A definative plan of action is an indicator.
   e. Unemployment increases the risk for suicide.

83. Who has developed a case arguing that mental health professionals do *not* have an absolute duty to prevent suicide?
   a. Jourard
   b. Glasser
   *c. Szasz
   d. Rogers
   e. Wubbolding

84. Under the case for suicide prevention which of the following is *false?*

    a. Once a counselor determines that a significant risk does exist, appropriate action must be taken.

    b. Failure to take action can result in the therapist's being held liable.

    *c. Consider decreasing the frequency of the counseling sessions, so as not to create dependency on the client.

    d. Develop a therapeutic contract with suicidal clients.

    e. Do not make yourself the only person responsible for the decisions and actions of your client.

85. Which of the following is *not* advisable when working with a suicidal client?

    a. increasing the frequency of counseling sessions

    *b. labeling the client as suicidal

    c. encouraging the client to call you in times of crisis

    d. bringing significant others into the client's social network, with his or her permission

    e. considering the use of medication

CHAPTER 6—Issues in Theory, Practice, and Research

86. The main purpose of the diagnostic approach is to

    a. make clients feel better.

    *b. allow the therapist to plan treatments tailored to the special needs of the client.

    c. identify a category for insurance payments to clients.

    d. protect the therapist from malpractice.

    e. provide an aura of professionalism for the therapist.

87. Which is an argument *for* diagnosis?

   *a. Diagnosis facilitates the selection of the most suitable form of therapy.

   b. Diagnosis can increase the chance of a malpractice suit.

   c. Diagnosis can rob people of their uniqueness.

   d. Diagnosis can lead people to accept self-fulfilling prophecies.

88. Which is an argument *against* diagnosis?

   a. Diagnostic classifications facilitate administrative tasks.

   b. Diagnosis enables therapists to make appropriate treatment plans.

   *c. Diagnosis can narrow the therapist's vision by encouraging the therapist to look for behavior that fits a certain disease category.

   d. Diagnosis is required by managed care systems.

   e. Diagnosis provides a framework for research.

89. Informed consent for research participants entails the element of

   a. competence.

   b. full information.

   c. comprehension.

   *d. all of the above

90. Perhaps the most basic ethical guideline for using tests is to

   a. use tests that will tell clients what they should do.

   b. encourage clients to believe in any tests they take.

   *c. provide objective measures that will help clients make better decisions.

   d. select the one best test for the client.

91. What is an accepted ethical guideline in terms of having social and personal relationships with clients?

    *a. Therapists are advised to avoid dual relationships with their clients.

    b. Friendships with clients always have positive results in counseling.

    c. Counseling a friend is beneficial to both people involved.

    d. Any form of social relationships with clients always damages the therapeutic relationship.

    e. These dual relationships are not only highly unprofessional and unethical, but also illegal in most states.

92. The practice of bartering psychotherapy for either goods or services

    a. is considered unethical by virtually all the ethical codes.

    *b. has the potential for conflicts.

    c. is generally an illegal practice.

    d. is always an attempt of the therapist to control the client.

    e. presents no problems if both the therapist and the client agree on bartering arrangements.

93. Which of the following is an example of a relationship that involves blending of roles, yet with clear beneficial potential?

    a. sex in the supervisory relationship

    b. forming friendships with former clients

    c. bartering

    *d. mentoring

    e. combining business ventures with therapy relationships

94. When there is potential for negative consequences arising from a dual relationship, it is the responsibility of the professional to

    a. secure the informed consent of clients and discuss with them both the potential risks and benefits of the relationship.

    b. consult with other professionals.

    c. seek supervision if the risk for harm is high.

    d. document any dual relationships in clinical case notes.

    *e. all of the above

95. Dual/multiple relationships are generally prohibited because

    a. these relationships are also illegal.

    b. such relationships always impair professional judgment.

    *c. there is a danger of exploiting the client.

    d. clients often misuse their power in the transference relationship.

    e. these relationships always entail a conflict of interest.

96. Concerning ethical standards on sexual intimacy in therapy,

    *a. virtually all of the professional organizations now have a specific statement condemning sexual intimacies in the client/therapist relationship.

    b. only the APA has specifically included sexual intimacy with clients as unethical.

    c. most professional organizations do *not* have a specific code condemning sexual intimacies in therapy.

    d. none of the existing codes have any definite procedures for filing and processing ethical complaints against therapists.

97. The rationale for the conviction that sexual relationships between a therapist and client is both unethical and professionally inappropriate is that

    a. doing so involves the abuse of the power that therapists have by virtue of their function and role.

    b. it fosters dependency on the client's part.

    c. the objectivity of the therapist is lost.

    d. clients are usually psychologically hurt by such practices.

  *e. all of the above

98. The legal sanctions against therapists who engaged in sex with their clients include

    a. being sued for malpractice.

    b. not being able to continue one's professional practice.

    c. having their licenses revoked or suspended by the state.

    d. being ordered to undergo therapy to resolve their own problems.

  *e. all of the above

99. Concerning nonerotic physical contact with clients, therapists of which orientation tend to make most use of this practice?

    a. behavior-modification

    b. rational-cognitive

  *c. humanistic

    d. psychodynamic

    e. systemic

100. If you become aware of unethical behavior on the part of a colleague, most codes of ethics state that

    a. the matter must be reported to the ethics committee immediately.

  *b. it is best to discuss the matter with the colleague.

    c. there is a need to ignore the situation, because taking any action may only make matters worse.

    d. it is mandatory to write a report describing the details of the unethical behavior in case of a lawsuit.

101. Concerning making referrals, therapists have an ethical responsibility
    a. to refer a client if they feel at all uncomfortable in the relationship.
    *b. to refer clients to other professionals when working with them is beyond their professional training.
    c. to refer a clients if they have not experienced the client's problem
    d. all of the above

102. Licensure assures the public that the licensee
    a. has undergone their own personal therapy.
    b. has completed maximum education and training.
    c. is thoroughly competent to practice in areas they advertise.
    *d. has met certain specific requirements in terms of education and training.

103. Most licenses
    *a. are generic in nature.
    b. specify the types of clients or problems the licensee is competent to work with.
    c. specify the techniques a practitioner is competent to use.
    d. ensure that practitioners will competently do what their licenses permit them to do.
    e. all of the above

104. Licenses and certifications
    *a. are designed to protect consumers.
    b. require applicants to be in personal therapy.
    c. generally rely on faculty recommendations to determine which applicant has met the standards of competence.
    d. are required only for therapists who have acquired a specialization.

105. All of the following are arguments for licensing, except for which one?

    a. The welfare of the consumer is better protected with the legal regulation than without it.

    b. Licensing allows the profession to define for itself what it will do and will not do.

    c. Licensing is designed to protect the public from ignorance about mental-health services.

    *d. Licensing decreases the chances that practitioners' services will be better distributed.

    e. Licensing upgrades the profession.

106. A weak point of mandatory continuing education is that

    a. legally professional organizations cannot require practitioners to acquire necessary hours.

    *b. professional organizations cannot require practitioners to be intellectually and emotionally involved in continuing education.

    c. professional organizations cannot monitor the quantity and quality of continuing education activities.

    d. it is impossible for organizations to specify approved continuing education activity as a basis for recertification.

107. A drawback of the peer review model is implied in which question?

    a. Will professionals volunteer as peer reviewers?

    b. Are peers able to competently be involved in a review process?

    *c. Who determines the quality of the peer reviewer?

    d. Can peers be objective?

108. Which of the following actions is inappropriate when a counselor feels that he or she is unqualified to work with a particular client?

    a. avoid initiating the counseling relationship

    b. terminate the relationship

    c. suggest appropriate alternatives

    d. provide a referral

    *e. attempt to counsel the client while seeking relevant expertise

109. Which of the following is *not* true about continuing education?

   *a. It is mandatory in every state when seeking relicensure.

   b. It keeps practitioners up to date with new research and knowledge in their area of specialty.

   c. It helps to sharpen one's counseling skills.

   d. Many professional organizations require it for recertification.

   e. Gaining professional competence is an on-going process.

CHAPTER 9—Issues in Supervision and Consultation

110. Which one of the following is *not* the responsibility of a clinical supervisor?

   a. Supervisors are responsible for the actions of their trainees.

   b. Supervisors must check on the trainees' progress and be familiar with their caseloads.

   c. Supervisors must inform trainees about the goals and process of supervision.

   *d. Supervisors must be willing to provide personal therapy to trainees when trainees have personal problems that affect their clients.

111. Legally, clinical trainees are *not* required to make their clients aware that

   a. they are trainees.

   b. they meet regularly for supervision sessions.

   c. their cases may be discussed in group supervision meetings.

   *d. their grade depends on their success with the client.

112. Supervisors who have sexual contact with trainees are

   a. engaging in dual relationships.

   b. opening themselves to legal liability for failure to provide adequate supervision.

   c. exploiting their power as supervisors.

   d. in violation of the codes of ethics.

   *e. all of the above

113. In the case of counselor educators who counsel their students, this practice is
    a. always unethical.
    b. illegal in most states.
    c. always the decision of the counselor educator and the student involved.
    *d. specifically mentioned in most of the ethical codes.

114. Under what circumstances should a therapist consult with colleagues or specialists?
    a. when a client complains of physical symptoms
    b. when facing an ethical problem
    c. when working with a client for an extended period of time and losing objectivity
    d. when there are apparent conflicts between legal and ethical aspects
    *e. all of the above

115. According to your textbook, consultants do *not*
    *a. have specific licensure requirements.
    b. need to be concerned with value issues and relationship issues.
    c. have an ethical obligation to be competent and trained in the area in which they are consulting.
    d. need to be aware of the rights of consultees.

116. Essential components of multicultural counseling include all of the following *except*

    a. counselors are aware of culture-specific methods of helping.

    b. counselors feel comfortable with their client's differing beliefs.

    *c. counselors avoid becoming involved in out-of-office interventions.

    d. counselors are aware of how their own biases could affect minority clients.

    e. counselors can send and receive both verbal and nonverbal messages appropriately.

117. Which of the following is *not* one of the trends toward multicultural awareness?

    *a. There is an increasing recognition of the universality and applicability of Western values for all cultures.

    b. There is a trend toward acquiring knowledge of culturally different clients and gaining experience in working with minority clients.

    c. There is a concern for adapting techniques and interventions in ways that are relevant for the culturally different client.

    d. There is a recognition that counselor self-awareness is as important as cultural awareness in multicultural counseling situations.

118. A sense of identity that stems from common ancestry, nationality, religion, and race is defined as

    a. culture.

    *b. ethnicity.

    c. minority group.

    d. multicultural.

    e. ethnic-sensitive practice.

119. The generic term that refers to many different cultural environments in a pluralistic society, along with the relevant theories and techniques in counseling practice, is defined as

   a. culture.
   b. ethnicity.
   c. minority group.
   *d. multicultural.
   e. ethnic-sensitive practice.

120. A category of people who have typically been discriminated against or subjected to unequal treatment is defined as

   a. culture.
   b. ethnicity.
   *c. minority group.
   d. multicultural.
   e. ethnic-sensitive practice

121. A broad definition that can be associated with a racial or ethnic group as well as with gender, religion, economic status, nationality, physical capacity or handicap, or sexual orientation is the term

   *a. culture.
   b. ethnicity.
   c. minority group.
   d. multicultural.
   e. ethnic-sensitive practice.

122. The term "cultural encapsulation" implies

   a. a multicultural awareness important for counseling practice.
   b. a level of hostility against values of minority groups.
   *c. stereotypical thinking and ignoring of cultural differences.
   d. respect for the multiplicity of cultural values in our pluralistic society.

123. Western culture places prime value on all but which one of the following?

    a. choice

    b. uniqueness of the individual

    c. self-assertion

  *d. interdependence

    e. strengthening of the ego

124. Eastern culture places value on all but which one of the following?

    a. losing of oneself in the totality of the cosmos

  *b. individuality

    c. inner enlightenment

    d. conformity

    e. security

125. The Western system stresses all of the following *except*

  *a. extended family structure.

    b. nonconformity.

    c. competition.

    d. freedom.

    e. conflict.

126. The Eastern system stresses all of the following *except*

    a. authoritarian orientation.

    b. collective responsibility.

  *c. nuclear family structure.

    d. collective actualization.

    e. compliance.

127. Which belief/attitude is *not* characteristic of the culturally skilled counselor?

    a. They can appreciate diverse cultures, and they feel comfortable with cultural differences.

    b. They are aware of their own values, attitudes, and biases and how they are likely to affect minority clients.

    *c. They are committed to the importance of persuading their clients to accept the values of the dominant society.

    d. They are willing to refer a client because of their limitations in cross-cultural counseling.

128. Which of the following knowledge is *not* characteristic of the culturally skilled counselor?

    a. They are aware of institutional barriers that prevent minorities from using psychological services.

    *b. They know all the diagnostic categories of DSM-IV as they apply to various minority groups.

    c. They understand the impact of oppression and racist concepts on the mental-health professions.

    d. They possess specific knowledge about the traditions and values of the group they are working with.

129. Which of the following skills is *not* characteristic of the culturally skilled counselor?

    *a. They understand that one counseling style can be used equally effectively with all minority groups.

    b. They are able to send and receive both verbal and nonverbal messages accurately and appropriately.

    c. They are able to make out-of-office interventions when necessary by assuming the role of consultant and agent for change.

    d. They are able to employ institutional intervention skills on behalf of their clients.

130. The ethics codes of ACA, APA, and NASW clearly state that discrimination is unethical and unacceptable on the basis of all but which of the following?

   a. race

   b. ethnicity

   *c. the counselor's level of education and training

   d. gender

   e. sexual orientation

CHAPTER 11—The Counselor in the Community

131. The community mental-health worker focuses primarily on

   a. the early crises in an individual's life and how they were resolved.

   * b. the person-in-the-environment.

   c. the quality of the bonding that took place between the child and the mother.

   d. using traditional approaches to bring about changes with at-risk clients.

   e. finding ways to include the family of origin in any individual's therapeutic plan.

132. The community counselor who works to empower disenfranchised groups such as the homeless, the handicapped, and AIDS victims illustrates

   a. direct community services in the form of preventive education.

   b. indirect community services aimed at changing the social environment by influencing policymakers.

   c. direct client services focusing on outreach activities to an at-risk population.

   *d. indirect client services of client advocacy involving active intervention on the behalf of an individual or a group.

133. Programs such as life-planning workshops, value-clarification seminars, and interpersonal-skills training are examples of

   *a. direct community services in the form of preventive education.

   b. indirect community services aimed at changing the social environment by influencing policymakers.

   c. direct client services focusing on outreach activities to an at-risk population.

   d. indirect client services consisting of client advocacy involving active intervention on the behalf of an individual or a group.

134. When counselors go into the community and develop programs to help clients deal with stressors that impair their coping ability, such as employee assistance and substance-abuse treatment, this illustrates

   a. direct community services in the form of preventive education.

   b. indirect community services aimed at changing the social environment by influencing policymakers.

   *c. direct client services focusing on outreach activities to an at-risk population.

   d. indirect client services consisting of client advocacy involving active intervention on the behalf of an individual or a group.

135. Counselors who attempt to change the social environment by transforming social policy illustrate

   a. direct community services in the form of preventive education.

   *b. indirect community services aimed at changing the social environment by influencing policymakers.

   c. direct client services focusing on outreach activities to an at-risk population.

   d. indirect client services consisting of client advocacy involving active intervention on the behalf of an individual or a group.

136. The trend toward the increased use of paraprofessionals means that

    a. mental-health professionals can be expected to spend more time in providing direct services to clients.

    *b. professionals will have to assume new and expanding roles.

    c. all direct services will be performed by paraprofessionals.

    d. the public is likely to get inferior services.

137. The system may be so cumbersome and difficult for clients to work with that counselors often need to assist their clients by adopting the role of

    a. consultant.

    b. advocate.

    c. adviser.

    d. facilitator of indigenous support systems.

    *e. all of the above

138. According to the authors, those practitioners who work within a system

    a. are almost certain to experience burnout.

    *b. are challenged to learn how to make the system work both for themselves and their clients.

    c. cannot remain in the system and also retain their integrity and dignity.

    d. must learn to take advantage of the system through manipulation of those in power.

CHAPTER 12—Ethical Issues in Marital and Family Therapy

139. Gender-aware therapy is primarily aimed at

    a. helping men and women to adjust to social norms of appropriate sex-role behavior.

    *b. helping clients understand how societal conceptions of gender often limit their thinking, feeling, and behaving.

    c. developing techniques to get women clients to become more assertive.

    d. encouraging clients to become politically involved in changing gender-based discrimination.

140. If counselors are working with families, and if their program did not prepare them for competence in family therapy, they are

   *a. vulnerable to a malpractice suit.

   b. doing what they must do under the circumstances.

   c. on safe ground as long as the family knows about their limited training.

   d. doing the appropriate thing if an individual client requests family therapy sessions.

141. An example of experiential methods of training in family therapy is

   a. listening to class lectures on family systems.

   b. observing family therapy sessions and taking notes.

   *c. working with one's own family of origin.

   d. doing readings in family therapy.

   e. none of the above are experiential.

142. The AAMFT *Code of Ethics* contains statements about each of the following areas except for

   a. confidentiality.

   *b. requiring personal therapy for family therapy trainees.

   c. professional competence and integrity.

   d. fees.

   e. responsibility to students, employees, and supervisees.

143. Regarding the matter of fees for professional services, the AAMFT codes specify that family therapists

   *a. do not accept payment for making referrals.

   b. do not become involved with third party payors.

   c. never change their fee structure during the time they work with a given family.

   d. must have clients sign a document that states that they understand the policies pertaining to payment for services.

   e. none of the above

144. Regarding confidentiality in the practice of family therapy, the authors contend that therapists should explain to the family

    a.   that there is no confidentiality within the structure of the family therapy sessions.

    b.   that all secrets must be disclosed.

    c.   that confidentiality of individuals is respected, if the information is obtained in a session with the individual alone.

    d.   that confidentiality does not apply in cases involving extra-marital affairs.

  *e.   their position on confidentiality from the outset of therapy.

CHAPTER 13—Ethical Issues in Group Work

145. The ASGW *Professional Standards for Training Group Workers* calls for

    a.   required individual therapy for trainees.

    b.   required group therapy for trainees.

  *c.   a minimum number of hours of supervised practice in leading groups.

    d.   achieving a passing score on an objective test on group counseling.

    e.   a doctorate in counseling psychology.

146. Concerning the matter of the psychological risks involved in participating in a group, ethical practice demands that leaders

    a.   make sure that their groups are risk free.

    b.   insist on members signing a contract stating they are willing to incur any potential risks or negative outcomes of a group.

  *c.   take precautionary measures to reduce unnecessary psychological risks.

    d.   consult with an attorney to determine if these risks might make leaders vulnerable to malpractice suits.

147. Which of the following is *not* considered an ethical issue related to an ongoing therapeutic group?

    a. the impact of the therapist's values on the group

    b. protecting members from unnecessary risks

    c. being alert for symptoms of psychological debilitation in group members

    d. maintaining confidentiality

    *e. making sure the group is homogeneous in population

148. Group leaders who fail to screen potential members for their groups are

    a. are highly unethical in all circumstances.

    b. are guilty of illegal practices.

    c. are behaving in highly unprofessional ways, and are likely to be sued.

    *d. more likely to include a group member who may not function well in the group setting.

149. Confidentiality in groups

    *a. is not protected by law in most states.

    b. can be legally assured if the group leader is a licensed professional.

    c. presents no ethical dilemmas.

    d. can be guaranteed for the members at the first session.

150. Involuntary group participation

    a. is clearly unethical.

    b. is always an invasion of the rights of clients.

    c. is illegal in most states.

    *d. can be ethical if informed consent procedures are followed.